KRISHNA CHARITAM

AN 18ᵀᴴ-CENTURY EPIC

Kunjan Nambiar

Translation by Ram Varmha

JAICO PUBLISHING HOUSE

Ahmedabad Bangalore Bhopal Bhubaneswar Chennai
Delhi Hyderabad Kolkata Lucknow Mumbai

Published by Jaico Publishing House
A-2 Jash Chambers, 7-A Sir Phirozshah Mehta Road
Fort, Mumbai - 400 001
jaicopub@jaicobooks.com
www.jaicobooks.com

KRISHNA CHARITAM
ISBN 978-81-8495-574-3

First Jaico Impression: 2014

introduction

In medieval India, a popular cult grew around the legends of Krishna, the eighth incarnation of Vishnu, who was worshipped as one of the divine trinity governing the universe.

The earliest extant stories of Krishna are found in the Sri Bhagavata Puranam, a holy script dating from around 200 BC. A voluminous book, it became popular among the people of India over the centuries and eventually, abroad as well. Its tales have since been translated, written about and re-written by many famous poets and scholars in many languages and forms. One such narrative is presented here.

Titled *Sri Krishna Charitam* (literally, The Story of Krishna), this epic poem was written by Kalakkathu Kunjan Nambiar (1705–70), a poet, performer and master satirist of Kerala. His text follows the story of Krishna in classical style, from the latter's birth and mischievous childhood, to his teenage pastimes with the milkmaids of Vrindavan and on to the many colorful, astonishing awe-inspiring adventures of his adult life.

The whole poem is composed in a mercurial literary style known as Mani-Pravalam, literally, Ruby-Coral. The name is a reference to the combination of Sanskrit (likened to a ruby) and Malayalam (coral) that was used in the composition of such poems and narratives.

During Kunjan Nambiar's time, Sanskrit, an Indo-Aryan language, was the exclusive domain of the erudite classes. Malayalam, with its Dravidian roots, belonged to the people. However, during the 16th- to 18th-century, Mani-Pravalam gained in popularity and became the favoured styled with many elite composers. It is easy to see why – the adroit use of words from both languages gives readers the impression that Mani-Pravalam is a distinct language of its own.

The translation presented here is a complete rendition of the original composition of Kunjan Nambiar. I hope that the beauty of its composition will quickly become apparent to readers. Kunjan Nambiar was very versatile in his composition and I have tried to make the English translation as true to the original as possible.

The translation is divided into 12 chapters of 70–90 verses each, bringing the total to some 912 stanzas in the form of couplets, quatrains and octaves.

This 18th-century text has never before been translated into English. It is therefore my hope that I am sharing the great pleasure that I find in this text with a wider public.

Ram Varmha
Kochi, Kerala
May 2014

contents

birth of lord krishna

1.1

Hail to Lord Ganesa; also to goddess Vaani,
Beloved of Brahma, born of the lotus,
Also to my mentor, the learned scholar,
Grant me thy blessings, to favour this work.

1.2

To Lord Siva, Destroyer of Cities; also to Lord Vishnu,
And, the Son of the two, Lord of the Bhutas,
To the learned Brahmins and people of knowledge,
Their blessings are sought, appropriately, as needed.

1.3

This is an epic, about Lord Krishna, - exquisitely set
With sweet words - as threaded, with 'rubies and corals',
May one's spiritual knowledge bloom like a lotus,
When reading from the few pages of this text.

1.4

Due to the wickedness of the evil Asuras,
And unable to bear the weight of their crimes,
Goddess Earth, to the abode of Brahma went,
With modesty and grace, her grievances to plead.

1.5

"Oh, Lord, born of the lotus, save me, save me,
With undue haste, Oh, God of Compassion – I pray,
Know, that I, the Earth, in deep depression lie,
Oh Lord, guardian of the worlds, thy help, I seek.

1.6

Here, with gods and noble sages so assembled;
A maiden, without apprehension,
Casting her thoughts, may seem inappropriate,
Yet, unending distress makes thy need to seek.

1.7

Though, without caution, these words I speak,
Oh Great Soul, kindly pardon my words;
Firm mountains may quake, but not so, I deem,
Great minds will quiver, by spurious words.

1.8

Hordes of Asuras, in human form,
Gory miscreants, under Kamsa's rule,

These, fearsome, worthless warrior gangs,
Roam freely on my land - Oh, mercy, mercy!

1.9

To thwart the rituals of pious Brahmins,
The eager villains have set about,
By goading the devil hordes to plot,
From day to next, such acts to perform.

1.10

Stealing cows, harming helpless dames,
Destroying pious Brahmins homes,
Such insidious crimes of equal means,
Evil men perform, without concern.

1.11

Like thunder claps they roar,
Their ugly words, unbearable to hear,
Full of wicked tales imbibed,
Quickly tame both men and beasts.

1.12

Tall mountains, forests, trees and shrubs,
Deep seas, where whales swim and play,
These are not heavy for me, Oh Lord,
But the weight of evil doers is hard to bear.

1.13

With thundering noise their evil army march,
And roam the realm, beyond control,
The dust blown up from the earth they trod,
The brightness of the solar orb is blanked.

1.14

By the riotous actions of their evil moves,
The armies of the gods are soon subdued.
Pretending to show they guard the land,
They merely cause havoc in their wake.

1.15

To alleviate my discomfort and my fear,
Brahma, born of the lotus, thy help I seek.
My past and future sorrows I need not repeat,
Oh, knowledgeable Lord, for you to hear.

1.16

Hearing these words of the Goddess Earth,
The kind and compassionate, Lord Brahma,
Smilingly and with sweet words said:
"Enough, enough - grieve not, divine Queen.

1.17

The Perfect Being, residing in the milky sea,
Lord Padmanabha, the Seat of Knowledge,

The lord of all, without doubt, will grant,
That wish you seek to ease your painful grief.

1.18

He, who is your beloved Lord and spouse,
Reclining on the serpent, protector of the world,
We, shall venture seeking help, from him,
To rid us from our grief – no need to fret.

1.19

Indra, Siva - the one who wears the noon -
Agni and Vayu, including the Vasus eight,
Other lordly and minor gods and I,
Will solemnly this journey make.

1.20

Come then, with undue haste, to the milky sea,
Where, bedding on the mighty snake,
He who sleeps in deep content and peace,
To Him, we'll humbly seek his help; proceed.

1.21

With His grace I have assumed, that role,
Of creator of these worlds, Oh, Goddess Earth,
Certainly, only at his lotus-like feet,
Lord Siva and I, seek salvation – none other".

1.22

So saying firmly did Lord Brahma,
With haste stood up from his lotus seat,
And with the many gods and Goddess Earth,
In tow, he quickly and gracefully, made to go.

1.23

To the shores of the milky sea, they went,
Indra and Brahma and other nobles too,
In haste, they proceeded with deep intent,
They went, singing praise to Lord Vishnu.

1.24

"Obeisance, to thee, Oh, lotus-eyed Lord,
We pray to thee, destroyer of evil, kind Lord,
Hail, hail to thee, Lord of all the worlds,
We pray to you of the colour of dark-cloud.

1.25

You cause the start and end of the universe,
You grant protection to all mankind,
You are endless, pure and infinite,
You guide the welfare of the lives of gods.

1.26

You are the being who is definable and not,
You are the essence of life to all life-forms,

You encompass those with or without blemish,
You are the Lord of all and of Lakshmi too.

1.27

Lord of all, manifested in endless forms,
Within this primordial cosmos, we behold,
Maya, mother of creation, by delusional ways,
With thy consent, this varied universe creates.

1.28

One may be rich; the other poor;
One may be cruel; the other kind,
Such varied types of men you mold,
O, Keshava, these creations you make.

1.29

Gigantic in size, was your form as the Fish,
Rugged indeed, was your form as the Turtle,
Strong in shape, was your form as the Boar,
Terrifying in sight was your Lion's form.

1.30

Afterwards, your form was as an ascetic,
Then, as Rama, you crushed the ruling clans,
You killed, the "Ten-Headed", as a Rama too,
Splendid are your forms, Lord of Bliss.

1.31

Destroyer of evil, protector of the meek,
Lord of the Universe, pray act, in haste.
To reduce the anguish of Goddess Earth,
What, kind Lord, would your answer be"?

1.32

Thus with sweet and praising words, they stood,
Honoured gods, with deep devotion merged,
Then, as thunder coming from darkened clouds,
A sound from the sky rang forth, for all to hear.

1.33

The meaning of the divine sound, was grasped,
By Brahma, the astute and clear minded soul,
And with sweet comforting voice conveyed,
Lord Vishnu's words, to the gods convened.

1.34

"Hark to these words, oh noble gods,
Kindly heed Lord Vishnu's declaration,
He will be born on earth, soon in time,
To the lofty lord Vasudeva, as his son.

1.35

The serpent Ananta will also take birth,
As the older brother of Vishnu's form,

To serve the two, offer your kind help,
And go take birth in Yadu's house.

1.36

Goddess Maya, the substance of this world,
Has kindly consented to be born on earth,
Go forth, now, you young goddesses to earth,
And assume various charming forms.

1.37

To lessen the burden of the Goddess Earth,
With haste, Lord Vasudeva will act.
Doubt not who his loved consort is,
Will he tarry long, her sorrow more to last"?

1.38

Hearing thus the words of Brahma,
Full of hope and impending fulfillment,
Goddess Earth, with greater joy departed,
So, the gods, in haste, proceeded.

1.39

Soon, hereafter, in the city of Mathura,
The calm, mild-mannered son of Surasena,
Noble Vasudeva, chief of the Yadava clan,
He with love sought the hand of Devaki.

1.40

Her hair was the colour of darkened clouds;
Her brother, the son of King Ugrasena,
The great Kamsa, whom his subjects feared,
He ruled the kingdom of Bhoja, ruthlessly.

1.41

He deftly leaped upon the chariot,
To drive the cart where the newly weds sat,
As wedding gifts: elephants, carts, horses too,
To the esteemed groom, Vasudeva, he gave.

1.42

Boom of kettle-drums and waves of fans,
Royal emblems such as canopies and whisks,
Soldiers in formation marching in joy,
Swiftly, they began to move in ecstasy.

1.43

Thereupon, they heard loud celestial words,
Coming from the sky in fearsome form,
"This woman's son, the eighth, mark you,
Great Kamsa, will cause your death, be sure."

1.44

Hearing these words, he with anger swelled,
The impetuous and furious Bhoja king,

Reached forth and held her sister's locks,
And he aimed his sword to cut off her head.

1.45

Then, the even tempered Vasudeva,
In a fearless yet rational way, approached,
"Do not - do not, execute a bride, great one,
For, in doing so, much sin will follow thee.

1.46

Is it honourable for you, Oh Lord to kill,
A woman, even be they worthless in esteem?
But, what past wrong did this maiden do?
Mercy, mercy, how heartless can you be?

1.47

For fear of losing your own life,
You chose to kill your own sister?
Your fame of being a fearless leader,
Will be lost because your fear of death.

1.48

Birth and death, to human beings alike,
Is common fate: of this there is no doubt,
Our day to die is written in our heads,
So destined, are we born on earth.

1.49

Some live on for greater time,
Some die sooner, following fate,
Death will come to pass for one and all,
You, with deeper wisdom, know so well.

1.50

Flesh and dirty refuse this carcass holds,
Worldly woes and sorrow fills this pot,
Such indeed, Oh King, is the state of man,
See how futile are your deep desires?

1.51

If helpless beings are put to death,
Then like thunderbolts will curses fall on thee,
And lead you to the darkest part of hell,
Thoughtful lord, need these your choices be?

1.52

By and by, as these unholy acts accrue,
The King of Bhoja will be held to blame,
No need to give support, let us vacate,
Saying so, your subjects will part from you.

1.53

'Kamsa is indeed of cruel mind',
So saying you will be vilified,

Attempt not, Oh King, to seek that fate,
Enough; curtail from such wanton acts".

1.54

Even after hearing all his pleas,
King of Bhojas, no kindness showed,
In response, after careful thought,
Vasudeva said the following words.

1.55

"Hear then this appeal, unlike in form,
Oh King, if your sister giving birth,
A son; with haste will I hand him to thee,
O King of the world, do not fret in vain".

1.56

Hearing these words of Vasudeva,
King of Bhoja, retired to his place,
And with her husband, Devaki went,
That she may live, at her home, in joy.

1.57

One hundred days thus having passed,
The beautiful Devaki so conceived,
And born to her was a beauteous son;
The virtuous always gain their wish.

1.58

Abiding his words, that honest man,
The father, gave the son to Kamsa's care,
Being pleased, Kamsa said:
"It is not in me to kill a new born child.

1.59

Kindly raise the boy under your care,
Later, I shall kill your eighth born child."
Thus Kamsa handed back the boy,
And Vasudeva took his son from him.

1.60

Then, Narada, the trouble causing saint,
Came to that wicked soul and said,
Do not; do not concede, O Bhoja king,
And show such weakness of your heart.

1.61

You, your creed, and all around,
Were born on earth as Asura folks,
But, the Vrishni and the Yadava clans,
Are come, from but the Deva group.

1.62

After, hearing the words of Narada,
The Bhoja king, grew much distressed,

That first born, healthy son, he took,
And he killed him, in a haughty mood.

1.63

A second son was born to Devaki,
Whom Kamsa quickly killed in style,
Thus, six more sons to Devaki born,
That fool destroyed, to save his neck.

1.64

Following the command of Vishnu,
Ananta, king of the serpents came,
As the seventh offspring, in the womb,
Of Devaki; he did appear so quickly.

1.65

Lord of Vaikunda, to Maya Devi, said:
"In Devaki's womb lies a soul, Oh Virtuous,
With undue haste pick up that soul,
It is there for the good of men.

1.66

Transfer the life-soul of great Ananta,
To the honourable Vasudeva's,
Senior wife - Rohini's womb,
And cause what was not intended, to occur.

1.67

The esteemed of the Gopa clan,
Is Nanda Gopa, and whose wife,
The most desirable damsel of them all,
Is Yasoda, and in her womb,
Take birth; you who ends rebirth and death.
Oh, goddess worshipped by one and all,
This will indeed be for the common good.

1.68

Following, the wishes of Vishnu,
Maya Devi did with joy,
Move the life-soul in Devaki's womb
And placed it in the womb of Rohini,
Then, she placed herself in the womb,
Of the beautiful, Yasoda,
And she waited patiently,
To be born, to her.

1.69

News of Devaki's miscarriage,
Echoed through the land,
People all over, on hearing this,
They became sad and despondent.
God of gods, Lord of all, Pure-of-State,
Unfathomable, Lord Achuta,
As worshiped by Devas and men -
You quickly made to Devaki's womb.

1.70

Then, Rohini, so beautiful of form -
Radiating with the glow of the moon,
Gave birth to a boy, so delightful,
That he was the envy of the world.
Gentle-people were so enwrapped,
At the mere sight of Rohini's son.
And the boy, moon-like in color,
Grew up, playing gleefully.

1.71

Blue-black clouds billowed and bellowed;
From the sky, abundant rain drops fell -
How beautiful was nature's revelry?
As mid-night neared, the moon appeared,
In all its sublime glory,
And celestial hymns were loudly heard,
From the sky, when the holy hour approached.

1.72

And, when the time of birth was near,
All the virtues of the worlds,
Combined in a totally blissful way,
And at the propitious moment of the blessed time,
Joining the astral confluence,
Of Astami and Rohini, was born -
Handsome like the darkened clouds -
Lord Krishna, the root of all the worlds.

1.73

He, with the shining gold crown, and bracelets, too,
Girdle, yellow robe and garland of flowers,
Holy Srivathsa mark and Kausthubha jewel,
Adorning the upper chest, between the arms,
Holding in his four hands, the conch,
The discus, the mace and the lotus flower,
May that Lord Vishnu, coloured like the clouds,
Grant you his blessings, infinite in scope.

childhood at ambadi

2.1

When Lord Krishna was born,
All the worlds began to glow,
Fragrance of the mango and celestial trees,
Was, wafted freely by the blowing breeze.

2.2

People every where were happy and content,
And flower petals rained from the sky,
Afterwards, when Krishna was born,
Women waiting birthing, in comfort lived.

2.3

Wearing the crown, ear-drops and necklaces,
And clothed in the yellow robe of silk,
He was seen to glow, holding in his hands,
The conch, mace, discus and the lotus flower.

2.4

Then, the sublime form of Vishnu,
Was visible in all the glory of the lord,
And seeing the glorious form of Vishnu,
Vasudeva, in chaste words, began to praise.

2.5

"Obeisance to thee, Oh, wielder of the bow,
I pray to thee, oh Krishna, protector of the weak,
Obeisance to thee, Oh Lord of the worlds,
I pray to thee, Oh Lord – Sea of Kindness.

2.6

Though ignorant was I of inner knowledge,
Knowledgeable, now am I due to your desire,
With depthless characteristics, have you,
Filled the worlds, and rules them accordingly.

2.7

You are like the glowing lamp,
That pervades the vastness of the universe,
You who are immovable, grant me quickly,
The protection I seek, without delay.

2.8

At first you created these entire worlds,
Then you maintain it with good care,

Later you destroy these worlds without a care,
Thus, you play these games dispassionately.

2.9

Watch the waters of the sea reflect,
The sky – and make believe it is the sky,
In such Illusion's ploys we see,
Thy directing hand so employed.

2.10

Lacking true knowledge within ones mind,
People in arrogance of ego live,
If one believes in your sacred tales,
His feelings change to endless bliss.

2.11

Material pleasures are the seat of woes,
But, chaste love is supreme knowledge,
Even the wise, without knowing this truth,
Find them sinking in the sea of life.

2.12

The sins committed in previous lives,
Make even the good, to be desire filled,
If one blends with thy inner self, then,
He is surely freed from illusory woes.

2.13

The type of evil men like Kamsa,
Will be destroyed by you in this birth,
Those of us with true devotion moved,
We will be saved, from worldly woes.

2.14

They were your brothers, pretty babies,
Born to me as my beloved sons,
With disdain they were killed by that devil,
Just like an eagle kills the snakes.

2.15

That Kamsa is equal to a lion in valour,
And destroyed the nations here and there,
If, now, he hears the news of your birth,
He'll surely come to harm you, Lord!

2.16

From this four-armed form, oh Lord,
Kindly revert to your former self,
If the guards of Kamsa takes this news,
Quickly, with hate, he will come to view."

2.17

Thereupon, Devaki too began to praise,
"Oh, noble Lord, I bow to thee; Oh God,

Destroyer of the wicked, have you come,
To be my son – glorious it is to know?

2.18

Oh, Lord, it is indeed my great fortune,
Also that of the Yadava clan,
You, of great wisdom and high respect,
Chose to come to earth for birth.

2.19

You who are the remover of worldly woes,
You who lie supine on the king of snakes,
You who is the root of all the Vedas,
May you bless for having lived inside of me."

2.20

Thus when the father and the mother too,
With great heartfelt devotion praised,
The lord, smilingly and with tender look,
And filled with love, He replied thus:

2.21

"My father, my mother, you are truly blessed,
You may live without fear or concern,
I, Vishnu, seeing your good nature,
Grant you my blessings whole heartedly.

2.22

Because, you, in your many previous lives,
Performed so many deeds of note,
This my glorious cosmic form,
You are fortunately blessed to view.

2.23

There is a devoted, noble lady of much fame,
The spouse of Nandagopa; Yasoda by name,
That genteel lady, lives in Gopa-land,
She rests, having birthed a baby girl.

2.24

In secret you should carry me from here,
Quickly, before that oaf discerns of this,
Lay me down in the house of Nandagopa,
And bring the girl-child from there to here."

2.25

Thus, Krishna, having said these words,
Assumed the form of a little child,
Kicking his feet he cried aloud,
And he laid down playing many pranks.

2.26

Gently, Vasudeva picked the baby up,
And he proceeded slowly, forth,

Black darkness reigned everywhere,
And dense was the forest, on the way.

2.27

Struck by the thundering rain from clouds,
Uprooted trees were falling down,
Flowing waters, breached the banks,
This caused the trees to fall to earth.

2.28

In the dead of night, those places on the path,
Hard to cross were made easy to advance,
The king of the cobras spread its hood,
And it served as a firm canopy from the rear.

2.29

Though the waves crashed to break the banks,
With the full waters of the river Kalindi,
The waters never even touched,
Vasudeva's feet by His grace.

2.30

At the cow-shed where Yasoda lived,
He placed the boy at her arms length,
Then he picked the baby girl, in his arms,
And he returned, with happiness in his mind.

2.31

When Yasoda woke up slowly,
She embraced her son so lovingly,
And in the sea of total bliss,
That beautiful woman was so involved.

2.32

Vasudeva, brought that baby girl,
And placed her next to his own wife,
With immense love that girl was held,
By Devaki, as she took her with much love.

2.33

At the time when Krishna was born,
The chain anklets that had fallen free,
Were reattached on their feet and hands,
And the couple lived in discomfort again.

2.34

Hearing the child's cries, those guards,
Four or five of them, went quickly forth,
To the harem where Kamsa was,
And they briefed him of the day's event.

2.35

Kamsa went forth with undue speed,
To do the killing at the site of birth,

Then Devaki full of grief,
Spoke thus with unending flow of tears.

2.36

"Do not kill my baby girl - my brother,
Is it good to kill women? But listen:
Not one, not two, but six baby boys,
Have you killed, without heart?

2.37

Even hearing the laments of his sister,
He scornfully, grabbed the baby girl,
And holding her by the feet,
He aimed to strike the rock, gleefully.

2.38

That nimble maiden, leaped off his hands,
And flew up to the realm where gods reside,
With such brilliance of far exceeding shine,
Like the doomsday orb of sun in glare.

2.39

With shining arms, four and eight by count,
Holding arms of brilliance, such as the spear,
With a blissful form whom sages pray to,
The Goddess Maya to Kamsa said:

2.40

"Oh Kamsa, thou, base and brutal fool,
Do not show thy prowess at women,
Your nemesis has already been born,
Quickly, search him every where.

2.41

Though you planned to strike my head,
You held my feet - there is no doubt;
Hence, I kill you not, but hark,
Thy killer is already born on earth."

2.42

Saying thus the goddess disappeared,
And Kamsa returned most befuddled,
To Vasudeva and his wife Devaki,
And he said to them, thus:

2.43

"I am a sinner and a savage too,
Certainly, to have killed my sister's sons,
No one in this world will grant me haven,
If in great apprehension I may live.

2.44

We are born and we die soon after,
Even the sages suffer body loss,

Even though I may have great inner fears,
I will never perform such cruel deeds again.

2.45

Be assured Oh, Devaki – that your sons,
Though now dead, should not worry you,
For one day our soul must surely part,
Glorious to die before old age comes on.

2.46

Like bubbles on the water's face,
Ephemeral is the bond of man to life,
Family, health, sons or wife,
They'll not grant peace when death is near.

2.47

Deaths, as based by ordained fate,
Blame not my killings as their cause,
Have we the right to over-pass,
When acts by divine plans are set?"

2.48

Kamsa, said such soothing words with love,
And the great one assumed a humble mode,
He untied the chains on their limbs,
And, light of heart, went to his abode.

2.49

At that time in Ambadi, with joy,
Nandagopa and his clan of Gopas lived,
Quickly, did the nobles of the land,
Gain the satisfaction to see Nanda's son.

2.50

Colored like the rain filled clouds,
With splendid black hair - envy of the bees -
Was seen to hang below the ears in length,
Those around were drowned in happiness.

2.51

With a face as radiant as the autumnal moon,
With a broad and splendid body shape,
From toe nail to his tuft of hair,
The baby's form was beautiful to behold.

2.52

When seeing that figure, so cupid-like,
The mind of Yasoda was overwhelmed,
Holding the baby close to her breasts,
She brought the child, for folks to see.

2.53

Nandagopa the most respected one on earth,
Gave donations to the esteemed souls,

Thousands in cows and gold he gave,
Thus, he granted quantities to those on earth.

2.54

After ablution, he performed the birth ceremony,
With flowing tears of greater joy,
At dawn he gathered all his kith and kin,
To show them his lotus faced son of his.

2.55

He decorated his entire residence,
To welcome the group of nobles of the land,
With gum, sandal and camphor scents,
And fruits and kinds of flower blooms.

2.56

Lamps were placed on the shining walls,
Sparkling ornaments were duly hung,
Cool saffron liquid was sprayed on ground,
And it was sprayed on the king's courtyard as well.

2.57

Thus, for five or six days, did Nandagopa,
Live happily in his home,
Finding it was time to pay Kamsa his levies,
He quickly ventured forth with some anxiety.

2.58

Reaching Mathura city with other Gopas,
He gave to Kamsa the annual dues,
On the way back, some happy days to fill,
He stopped at Vasudeva's place to rest.

2.59

Overwhelmed with over flowing joy,
Vasudeva said these words, with happiness:
"The blessings of my past life is not done,
I have this chance to see you once again.

2.60

Hark, my friend, God has granted you,
With blessings beyond compare,
To live happily by seeing your son's face,
That which is one's right has come to you.

2.61

Rohini's and my son, Balarama,
Is he not living in your house?
The boy and his mother live in your house,
All they seek is your kind heart.

2.62

Heed then these words,
Equal to the worst of hearing,

A black enchantress by name Putana,
She has taken to killing little children.

2.63

Proceed then, with due haste to your house,
Tarry not lest it may bring you misery,
When the enemies are growing in great strength,
Can one maintain much peace of mind"?

2.64

When Vasudeva said such thoughtful words,
Nandagopa, grew fearful hearing them,
Concerned that some evil may come his way,
He went to his abode with Vishnu's blessing.

2.65

At that time, Kamsa's ego grew,
With Asura throngs, of opportunistic trends,
All of them, evil minded folks,
They quickly prospered on this earth.

2.66

To kill young boys, with no disdain,
Putana began to roam, from town to town,
Taking the form of a beautiful seductress,
She finally came to Krishna's place.

2.67

The overly clever woman came forth,
And slowly and gently picked up Govinda,
Playfully, she began to feed her large breasts,
Hark now, her death was not that far.

2.68

The boy-child grasped her heavy breasts,
And sucked the life blood out of her,
With a cry that equals the thunder clap,
She felled down, quaking the very earth.

2.69

On her chest, large as a granite rock,
Young Krishna was seen to lie,
The dark skinned Krishna was seen to play,
As he, in playful mode, moved his limbs about.

2.70

Yasoda, along with the Gopa women,
With trepidation, relief and anxiety,
Picked up Krishna in her hands,
And she embraced him from head to toe.

2.71

The hideous, huge body of Putana,
Was cut to pieces by an axe,

And burned completely in the fire,
That caused a pleasant odor to spread about.

2.72

Beautiful was she, as her curse was gone,
And she lived for ever in heavenly bliss.
Hark: Who reads Putana's salvation tale,
He will surely gain everlasting joy.

iii

krishna's frolics

3.1

Then, the body of the boy, Gopala,
Was from toe to head, sublimely beautiful,
Seeing this form, and in ecstatic joy,
The Gopa folks lived happily.

3.2

Sakatasura in the form of a cart,
Came to run over the body of Mukunda,
Effortlessly, the boy struck him with his foot,
And it fell apart into many broken parts.

3.3

The cloud-colored child who had with his feet,
Broken the cart, was picked up gently,
And reciting your names as best she could,
Yasoda lived with out further anxiety.

3.4

Soon thereafter, an Asura, named Trinavarta,
Came forward in the form of a whirl-wind,
Destroying forests and crumbling hills,
With great ferocity, he shook the earth.

3.5

With blowing dust he darkened the land,
And with great force the whirl-wind came,
To carry Narayana - what a fool -
And without hesitation he lifted him high.

3.6

Krishna, held him by his throat,
And as he squeezed his neck,
That hill-sized Asura's soul departed;
And he fell down to earth and died.

3.7

Like an Asoka bud lying on,
A mighty mountain side,
Did that crafty boy's charming form,
Lay on that Asura's chest.

3.8

Yasoda with great anxiety,
Went to gather the baby-boy in her arms,

Mindful it to be the blessings of the God,
That lovely woman lived in peace.

3.9

At that time, the great sage, Garga,
Came by to meet Vasudeva's needs,
And named Balabadra and Acuta -
Rama and Krishna, as chosen to suit.

3.10

As the famous boys played in Ambadi,
And slowly, grew joyously in that place,
People gained great happiness,
And prosperity reigned in the land.

3.11

No where on earth was misery seen,
Sorrow due to poverty had disappeared,
The fear of thieves had vanished,
And women never lost their chastity.

3.12

As the two boys grew up in Ambadi,
The Devas in heaven grew ecstatic,
But, the heart of Kamsa with malice grew;
Slowly he began to lose his confidence.

3.13

Those Gopa damsels seeking Krishna,
Would hand him, from one maiden to next,
Like a honey-bee that flies between,
A lovely flower bloom to another.

3.14

The two boys, gaining strength,
Began to crawl on the floor,
Frolics of these two, leaders of the worlds,
What ever it was a joy to behold.

3.15

Lord Mukunda, the dark-skinned one;
Lord Balarama, of crystalline hue,
These two together were like the rivers,
Kalindi and Ganga merged in flow.

3.16

With both their arms and knees,
Placed on the ground, they wandered about,
Those who saw them, with their smiling faces,
They knew not the limit to their inner joy.

3.17

The toddlers would stand up, by holding,
But, lacking comfort would fall,

Walk a few feet, gropingly,
Then fall on the ground and roll.

3.18

With jingling golden waist-belt,
Anklets making pleasant sounds,
And moving about playfully,
They charmed the houses of the Gopa clan.

3.19

The boys, went on, step by step,
And began to walk so gradually,
Quickly they would reach Gopa homes,
And they frolicked in their midst.

3.20

They ran around in the court-yard,
They leaped about with happy laughter,
They sang songs in such wondrous tone,
They danced to chorus; those noble souls.

3.21

Then, Krishna with much keen desire,
Get to the milk and butter with deceit,
Can one ascertain the reason why?
The Lord of Lords plays such pranks?

3.22

Slyly, with some friends in tow,
The clever Madhusudana would go,
To four or five houses and from there,
Steal all the milk to drink it full.

3.23

When the women go for their bath,
Krishna would sneak inside the house,
And having drunk much milk,
Splash some down and stand laughingly.

3.24

Those clay pots hung beyond his reach,
He, tap-holed them with a churning stick,
And as the milk gushed down from above,
With mouth wide open, he would drink it all.

3.25

With less warning, the boy would steal,
All the butter and eat the lot,
And if some remain he would feed the cat,
Such frolics he continued to do.

3.26

He would leap to grab the hanging pots,
And with gusto drink the milk and sour milk,

When the Gopa women came to know,
He would scamper home and hide from view.

3.27

Once, unable to bear, no longer,
The naughty pranks, of the Lord of Lords,
The Gopa women with angry displeasure,
Went to Yasoda, and stated their woes.

3.28

"Lady of the House - we are in deep trouble,
Your son's naughtiness grows endlessly,
Honestly, we find it troublesome to live,
From day to day, our grievances increase.

3.29

Those children who are prone to naughtiness,
Be whipped or punished as they grow up,
If you cannot hold his naughty ways,
How then can we be deemed to subdue him?

3.30

Thinking these pranks are merely plays,
And by spoiling him you lose the chance,
To right the wrongs as he grows up –
Hark; we will now narrate the episodes.

3.31

Your son, has plans to steal,
Dairy food without delay,
He is never satiated with what he gets,
Listen then to the woes of the Gopa dames.

3.32

The clever boy gets into people's homes,
And breaks their pots and jars,
Not only does he wander aimlessly,
Here and there, but destroys too.

3.33

This boy wants more than what he gains,
And, destroys the pots he holds as well,
To do these most naughty deeds,
This Krishna is indeed capable.

3.34

When this boy, comes seeking,
With greed, milk, ghee and sour milk,
We hand him these most generously,
But, over that he steals and eats as well.

3.35

Gopa maidens would never gripe,
To give what the young boy wants,
Those pots obtained with much effort,
When destroyed is such a loss to bear.

3.36

Those milk-maids who make a daily living,
By selling milk are most distressed;
Those who have known the pangs of penury,
Truly they will know the sufferings of the poor.

3.37

These are not just common pots to us,
They are like golden pots in use,
Prevailing sorrow due to loss of wealth,
That's equal both to rich and poor, alike.

3.38

The boy takes copper plates and water pots,
And lo, breaking, throws them in the dirt,
Those items that he sets his eyes upon,
Soon disappears from view – how sad it is!

3.39

It is known that for the Gopa-maids
Dairy food is their basic wealth?

The income that flows from daily chores,
What profit then - if all curtailed?

3.40

What can we do, if these boys,
Of royal lineage, resort to stealing?
Oh, lovely lady, due to this boy,
Everlasting ill-fame will fall on you".

3.41

Then, spoke up a Gopa maid,
"Your son is indeed a miscreant,
Listen, to a naughty deed, he did,
When, he entered my house that day.

3.42

For my aged father, I had warmed,
Some measured cups of milk,
Krishna drank all that milk,
And he filled the pot with water.

3.43

At days end, when darkness prevailed,
My father took a sip and then in rage,
He cried: 'You are cruel', and broke the jar,
And he threw it straight at me.

3.44

At that time this boy came over,
Laughingly he called out and said:
'Since you never gave me milk, last time;
This is vengeance' – Pray, what can I do"?

3.45

Immediately, another Gopa maiden said:
"Hark: the woes befell me are great by far;
Once, during dusk, treading quietly,
He entered my abode, without a word.

3.46

Those cows, milked and corralled,
Were let loose by him at night,
Quietly and in secret,
He drove them, to the fields near by.

3.47

Letting the cattle eat the ripened grains,
This boy left the scene, quietly,
And, early in the morning hours,
Unwarily, I went to milk the cows.

3.48

I stood looking for the missing cows,
Dearer to me than my life,

Then, I saw Krishna walking by,
And that boy had a jovial demeanor.

3.49

The cows were grazing in the field,
And the calves were there along with them,
'Silly woman, you may now milk the cows',
So saying, Krishna, left the scene.

3.50

Another damsel said with grief,
"Hard indeed it is to recount my woes;
The boy is mostly ill-behaved,
And full of pranks, as well - Yasoda!

3.51

I had filled the pots, full with milk,
And placed them on the hearth,
At that time this cunning boy,
Came and sat in my kitchen.

3.52

When I just went outside,
To gather some fire-wood,
This boy broke all the pots, with,
A churning-stick and, swiftly ran away.

3.53

Rather than having ill-mannered children,
Be it not better not to have them at all,
Due to the curse of gods, we are not,
Enjoying any form of happiness.

3.54

Should we forgive or should we seek,
And find a new place and settle in?
Will our misfortune ever end?
Will you help us, oh, Lady of Good-Heart"?

3.55

All these words of the Gopi maids,
Yasoda, heard with much respect,
Her deep attachment to her son in mind,
That elegant lady replied in a controlled way.

3.56

"Hearing the pranks of my son today,
I too am sorrowed inwardly,
Yet, to punish him for his mischievous acts,
Is far beyond me, oh, Gopi maids.

3.57

My fondness for him lies within,
Dislike me not on that account,

When loss by damage comes ones way,
Anger follows without doubt.

3.58

For loss of pots, of common clay,
I give you gold or jeweled ones,
Accept then my gifts of wealth,
Be satisfied; to your homes, retreat".

3.59

Thus saying, and with much reverence,
Wealth was distributed in great style,
And having cooled their hearts,
They were sent home with great care.

3.60

"Look, Krishna has eaten sand,
He surely will with illness fall",
With great anxiety and anger too,
Hearing such words, Yasoda came.

3.61

When he heard his mother remark,
"Shame, my boy; open up your mouth;
Let me see"; and Krishna, that illusionary,
Opened wide his mouth at her command.

3.62

When Yasoda looked into his mouth,
She saw, nether, earth and heaven too,
She saw, ghosts and ghouls and spirits too,
She saw, in his mouth, their troupes as well.

3.63

She saw forests and the seven mounts,
She saw lands and rivers and the seven seas,
She saw swaying snakes and human groups,
She saw leaping herds of animals.

3.64

She saw, the milky sea; the king of snakes;
She saw supine on it - in an illusory state,
The dark and blissful form of Vishnu there;
She saw, the four-headed Brahma too.

3.65

She saw demons; birds and tigers too;
Trees; vampires; dwellers of the caves;
Stars; warriors and their opponents;
In excess numbers, she saw them all.

3.66

She saw the Gopas and the Gopis, too;
The entire Gopa clan and just not that,

The cattle and their calves and more,
She even saw Govinda eating sand, in there.

3.67

Seeing thus these many things,
The Gopa lady was overcome with fear,
But, when she blinked her eyes again,
All she saw just disappeared!

3.68

Yasoda, the lady of good fortune,
Breast-fed Krishna and embraced him,
Recalling that he is her beloved son,
She forgot the happenings of the past.

3.69

While Yasoda was churning curds,
Vasudeva, at play, broke the pot,
With great anger, and in haste,
The mother moved to have him tied.

3.70

All the lengths of ropes brought forth,
Were seen as short by couple splits,
Yasoda grasped not the illusion here,
Since she too was by delusion ruled.

3.71

Wanting not to trouble his mother,
The master of illusion let it happen,
Easy now to tie him to a mortar stone,
Yasoda roped him thus and went away.

3.72

Because he was tied around the waist,
By a rope, Krishna was called Damodara,
Dragging the mortar stone, ever so slowly,
Rama's brother was seen to crawl away.

3.73

Standing, were a pair of lofty pines,
And towards the trees he made his move,
Dragging the mortar, past the trees,
The lotus-eyed-boy turned around.

3.74

As the trees toppled down flat,
There arose, two divine beings,
Knowing the story of Krishna,
The sons of Yaksha king spoke thus:

3.75

"Hark, Krishna, I am Nalakubara,
And this is Manigreva, behold,

We are the sons of the wealthy Kubera,
We always lived our lives in happiness.

3.76

Once, we consumed too much intoxicants,
Became blinded to an amorous mode,
By the shores of Ganga, with many maids,
We began to sing and dance passionately.

3.77

As we stayed in nude, enjoying love,
There came upon the sage Narada,
With great anger he cursed us both,
And by its strength we became trees.

3.78

The sage gave us pardon from his curse,
'When the son of Nanda touches you,
You will be fine and your hardship end',
That sage's words have now come true.

3.79

You are remover of grief, and lord of all,
You are pure of mind, and without form,
You are without beginning, and unexampled,
You are without end, our obeisance to you'.

3.80

Thus in humility and in praise,
The noble sons of Kubera left,
Those men who know these tales,
They will gain great peace of mind.

3.81

Hearing the cracking noise of the falling trees,
And startled at the sound there from,
The Gopas gathered there with anxiety,
And as they stood staring, they saw in form,
Most pleasing to Lakshmi; of one who grants,
Blessings to the lords of the eight worlds;
That master of illusion and in some distress,
He came dragging, the mortar-stone.

3.82

The ever loving father, Nanda Gopa, came forth,
To remove the bondage, from Krishna -
The one who removes worldly bondage -
And he then embraced the boy lovingly;
Nanda Gopa lived, amidst,
And in company of the cow-herdsmen,
They with close family ties;
With great happiness and joy.

days in vrindavana

4.1

Thereafter, in the land of the cow-herdsmen,
With such ill-omens accruing,
Nanda Gopa began to worry deeply:
Would it be proper to live here any more?

4.2

A close friend of Nanda came to him,
And spoke these kind words to him,
"There is a place, where, certainly,
We can live, in total peace and harmony."

4.3

There is a serene place, for sure,
Called Vrindavana, a land of prosperity,
Near the wondrous mount Govardhana,
That reaches to touch the clouds.

4.4

It will be most gracious to live,
On the sandy banks of Kalindi river,
It is my humble advice,
That we may all go there forthwith.

4.5

Then the many cow-herdsmen,
With excitement, began preparations,
Seated on carts and with merriment,
They began their travel, with much joy.

4.6

Amidst the young and old Gopas, together,
Herds of cattle, and lotus-eyed Gopi maids,
The most beautiful Yasoda and also Nanda Gopa,
They all gathered swiftly there, to journey forth.

4.7

The cow-herdsmen built their homes,
By the shores of the serene, River Yamuna,
And it seemed to them that, here on Earth,
There is no better place to live.

4.8

One day, Rama and Krishna,
Drove a large herd of little calves,

With much merriment and fun,
To graze in the deep wooded glen.

4.9

Adorned with arm-bracelets,
Fully clad with shining gold waist-band,
With peacock feathers in his hair,
Krishna went forth looking glamorous.

4.10

Shaking anklet charms and arm bracelets,
With sweet tones from the flute emanating,
And with playful smile and darting eyes,
The sweet tempered Krishna walked slowly.

4.11

Like the clear sun-stone in body hue,
Wearing a beautiful, shiny, blue silk garb,
With the demeanor of one of confidence,
He walked on slowly - the son of Rohini.

4.12

With compatriots of equal nature,
They with gaiety moved under the trees,
Grazing the cattle and moving intently,
They looked like the bright mid-day sun.

4.13

Drinking the water from the Yamuna,
To quench the weariness from the trip,
And, in the beautiful forest,
Playfully, engaged, they stayed.

4.14

To ambush the young boy Krishna,
An agent of Kamsa, in a heifer's form,
A wicked Asura came forth,
And he set about to do bodily harm.

4.15

The Lord of Kindness, knew early, the ploy,
And grabbed its feet with his hands,
And dashing it against a tree stump,
The Lord of the Worlds killed the evil one.

4.16

Gods dropped flowers from the sky,
To honour the Lord of the Worlds,
Krishna, seven-times handsome, Lakshmi's own,
Went to his abode, took food and slept.

4.17

When the sun dawned in the sky,
Vasudeva, woke up and bathed,

Taking some light food gently,
He was prepared to travel to the woods.

4.18

Yasoda called him to her side,
And caressed him gently and lovingly,
She undid his hair knot and tied it again,
And she later stroked his lotus face.

4.19

Adorning him with bracelets on both hands,
Tiger-rings around the neck,
Jingling waist-belt around the waist,
And she placed fragrant flowers on his hair.

4.20

Placing jeweled anklets on both feet,
She prepared Krishna for the trip,
She dressed Balarama also,
Quickly, and readied him lovingly.

4.21

Holding in his hand the horned flute,
And also the flute and the bent cattle prod,
Krishna started forth, with the Gopa boys,
To drive the cattle calves in front of them.

4.22

To play on the forest path,
He proceeded, with his elder brother,
And the dust from their lotus feet,
Made the woods much sanctified.

4.23

The dust from the feet of Krishna,
Made the forest land sublime,
Dew drops covered flower beds;
And bees began to sip the nectar-juice.

4.24

Peacocks and nightingales in joy immersed,
Rabbits and deer in play performed,
Mountains and fields and trees and grass;
Stags and boars in lively mood, enjoyed.

4.25

Lion and the elephant forswore their enmity,
The tiger and the swine behaved like one,
The cobra and the mongoose stayed level,
When, in the woods, Krishna remained.

4.26

An Asura, assumed the form, of a heron,
And with evil thought in his mind,

With claws and beak and thrusting eyes,
Like a mighty mountain, he looked.

4.27

With its beak like a cavern, outstretched,
It swallowed Mukunda (Krishna) whole,
But it could not hold his fire-like body,
And it released him from its mouth.

4.28

When returning to peck again,
Krishna held the demon's beaks by hand,
Tearing the Asura's beak by the middle,
He threw the pieces to either side.

4.29

On the head of the destroyer of the monster.
Flower blossoms, from the divine tree fell,
Showered by the gods in their happiness,
And people all over, gratefully rejoiced.

4.30

Thereafter, the boy spent the night,
In his own home, with his companions,
And in the morning, with his friends,
He proceeded to the woods, to do his chores.

4.31

Bagging a handful of rice, to eat,
And with it some salted condiments,
The cow herdsmen were excited,
And they were ready to help Krishna.

4.32

Maghasura, the python demon,
Laid in wait; his mouth wide open,
Assuming it to be an opening to a cave,
The Gopa group walked quickly inside.

4.33

Many had collapsed from the effects,
Of the poisonous heat from within,
And he who bears the banner of Garuda,
Krishna, too, decided to venture forth inside.

4.34

The python closed its mouth,
To end the life of the Lord-of-the-World,
Krishna, assumed a gigantic form,
And he tore its throat and killed it.

4.35

Then, from the body of Maghasura,
A form of brightness sprang forth,

When this merged with Krishna's form,
The gods in heaven cheered.

4.36

The youth, who was to women attached,
Ate the rice balls offered by the damsels,
Seeing all the frolics of Krishna,
Brahma seemed greatly astonished.

4.37

So, he made the calves disappear; then,
He made the mighty Gopas vanish too,
Brahma, as a means to test,
He posed to deceive the Supreme Lord!

4.38

Then Krishna, quickly, and effortlessly,
Created the same cows and herdsmen, too,
And a year thus passed between, and then,
Brahma appeared in front, in form.

4.39

The distinction between those of Brahma's,
And those that came of later creation,
Were not clear, and thus confused,
Brahma, the cause of all this, stood deluded?

4.40

Gopas and the cows Krishna created,
Turned to the form of Lord Vishnu,
With armlets, tiaras, and towering crown,
Waist-band, flower garland and yellow robe.

4.41

Pretty ear-drops in dolphin's shape,
Famed Kaustubha gem; mark of Srivatsa;
And shining in their four arms, beheld,
Discus, conch, mace and the lotus flower.

4.42

He, the son of Devaki was seen,
As one amongst those multi forms,
Seeing him, and with true devotion,
Brahma sang these hymns to him.

4.43

"You make the static worlds to stir,
You are the shining cosmos of Brahman,
You are he who in visible form reside,
You are he who invisibly resides, as well.

4.44

You are the one, who creates,
Multitudes of cows, birds and animals,

You are the one, who tracks them far,
And then ends their lives in due time.

4.45

Your inner body, in proper form contained,
All the movable and immovable worlds,
And it was you, oh Lord Vishnu,
We know, lying in cosmic sleep on the vast waters.

4.46

Life, death, calamity, arrogance of wealth,
Illness, gain in fortune, such as these,
That cause anxiety, are brought on by you,
Oh Lord, through the mysterious Illusion.

4.47

Seeds planted in the ground,
Sprouts forth branches and twigs,
Some break and fall; others bear fruits,
All this be but pre-ordained.

4.48

Thereafter, a wild fire may pass,
And burn to ashes the growing tree,
This, is the fate of all living things,
Wellness or losses are thy desire.

4.49

Hark; forgive me for my acts,
Performed with improper intent,
I who am capable of granting help,
I granted none to you.

4.50

To test the strength of your 'avatar',
I affected illusion to make things disappear,
I know now that you are truly great,
Beyond that I know not of?

4.51

This much is known here and just this:
Due to the past deeds of doe-eyed-maiden,
You were born, in form, as a deity,
In quality, you are like a sea of kindness".

4.52

Hearing the words of Brahma, Madhava,
Most pleased, blessed him so,
He made the numerous forms to end;
Once again he took the youth-like form.

4.53

Brahma, prostrated to the playful boy,
As he was standing with a morsel of food,

Then Brahma quickly disappeared,
And Krishna went to his abode.

4.54

Once, Krishna, with Balarama,
Went quickly to the Palmyra woods,
In measured happiness did Krishna seem,
With the Gopas and the cows, he went.

4.55

There, the cow-herdsmen began to eat,
The fruits fallen while shaking the trees,
Hearing of this, Dhenuka, was angry;
That Asura appeared in a donkey's form.

4.56

Balarama, the protector of the worlds,
Slew the monster Dhenuka in battle,
Then, the Asura's fraternal group,
In great anger drew close to do harm.

4.57

They assuming the forms of jackals,
Gave battle, deeply enjoying the tussle,
Balarama and Krishna jointly,
They killed all the Asuras in battle.

4.58

After eating the Palmyra fruits,
The lord-of-lords left for his abode,
Later, alone, without his brother,
He went to graze the cows, in the woods.

4.59

Hearing that in one place of Kalindi,
The waters were on fire with venom,
From the king of snakes, Kaliya,
He proceeded quickly there to see.

4.60

Cows and Gopas, drank the waters,
And fell dead at the river shore,
But, Krishna with his graceful glances,
Brought the fallen back to life.

4.61

Birds that fly above that place,
Had their wings singed and fell below,
Beasts like buffalos, elephants and such,
After drinking the waters dropped dead.

4.62

Krishna, who is kind at heart,
Was moved to sorrow at the sight,

Climbing on a mangrove tree,
He stood boldly at the top.

4.63

That tree burned by poisonous fumes,
Came back to life, with fresh bloom,
Enjoying his escapades,
Krishna leaped into the Yamuna waves.

4.64

As Krishna was playing gently,
And in the rolling waves, frolicking,
The king of snakes, with much anger,
Coiled him, bit and struck his body, hard.

4.65

The Gopa clan, standing on the sandy shore,
Saw the torments of the wide-eyed lord,
Seeing this, they were made to cry aloud,
And they stood by watching helplessly.

4.66

Seeing bad omens: Nandagopa,
The cow-herdsmen and women folks,
Along with Balarama, they came,
And pleaded to end this harmful game!

4.67

Freeing himself from the serpent's coils,
Vasudeva, effortlessly reached the shores,
Climbing atop the many hoods of the snake,
He began to dance in gallant style.

4.68

Anklets and bracelets jingled,
In rhythm with the steps of his feet,
To the tunes of wondrous songs,
His handsome face was dear to watch.

4.69

The hair on his head waved,
The peacock feathers in his hair quivered,
The bright colored yellow silk robe,
That fluttered with such grace.

4.70

Holding in his hand the glorious,
Flute that brings forth melodious tunes,
And pressing to his sweet lips on his face,
He played high pitched harmonious cords.

4.71

Thereupon, the gods residing in heaven,
Began their praise in melodious songs,

Drum, cymbal and tambour beats ran high,
And with true devotion they stood in awe.

4.72

Soon after, with boundless joy,
The heavenly maidens began to dance,
Kaliya, the king of snakes, began to tire,
The heavy weight caused his hoods to droop.

4.73

All the wives of the king of snakes,
With humility, they repeatedly implored,
Hearing the holy words and Vedic chants,
Vasudeva was quickly pleased.

4.74

Climbing off the hood of the serpent,
Gopala, with extended joy,
And stroking the king of serpents,
Krishna, said these words:

4.75

"Hark! Oh, king of snakes,
You will remain devoted towards me,
Vacate then the waters of Yamuna,
And with your family proceed elsewhere.

4.76

In the midst of the tranquil sea,
A place called Ramanam exists,
Kaliya, go that wonderful place,
And you will gain much happiness.

4.77

Oh Kaliya, of humble disposition,
Be not be fearful of, Garuda,
When he sees my foot prints on your hood,
Will he turn to be your enemy"?

4.78

Hearing this, he prostrated,
And the king of snakes was most satisfied,
The snake maidens gave to Krishna,
Many jewels and silk, and then departed.

4.79

The lotus blossoms closed their looks;
Soon after; when the sun began to set,
The Chakrakava goose, parted from its mate,
And water lilies opened cheerfully.

4.80

Total darkness now engulfed the world,
The timid retreated to their homes,

The love-seekers began to journey forth,
In secrecy, they sought passionate love.

4.81

Cupid, quickly bent his bow,
And gathered arrows in readiness,
For the chaste women waiting to,
Meet their husbands coming home.

4.82

When the happy day ended,
The knowledgeable son of Vasudeva,
Along with his parents, brother and others,
He began to ready to start their trip.

4.83

"Let all of us stay here thus,
There is no time to reach our abode",
Hearing from Krishna to stay in the woods,
The Gopas gladly agreed to follow suit.

4.84

At that time, from four sides, rose a dark,
Smoke, like a horde of black bees,
And a tall wild fire, with a blowing wind,
Was seen burning in the woods,

Animals like tigers, lions, boars,
And buffalos, were burned to death,
Swiftly, and burning furiously,
The fire came to Nanda and his folks.

4.85

As the great fire approached,
The people cried: Oh; how sad;
Mercy; we will soon be burned -
So, they cried with fear,
And when the Gopas began to faint,
Then, Krishna, who is the seat of love,
Came forth and that flaming fire,
Which destroys all, he swallowed.

4.86

As the agony caused by the fire ended,
Sun rose gloriously, over the eastern hill,
Krishna, happy with the Gopa's company,
Went home and lived happily.

adoration of the gopis

5.1

In due course, Rama and Krishna,
Passed past the age for games and play,
When the time will come, to please the fickle maids,
They would enjoy the inner passions of love.

5.2

Krishna and Rama, taking the heifer cows,
Reached the famous fig-tree – Bandera,
There Krishna and Balarama,
With their companions, they began to wrestle.

5.3

"He who loses the contest,
Must carry the victor on his shoulders",
Having thus agreed, the boys,
And others set to combat under a banyan tree.

5.4

An Asura named Pralamba, took the form,
Of a cow-herd and joined the combat,
He lost the tussle with Balarama quickly;
Still with arrogance he carried him on his back.

5.5

Assuming the Asura's form, carrying the load,
He took to the skies and began to run,
Thereupon, Balarama, using his fists,
Punched the Asura and killed him.

5.6

At that time, the cattle wandered far away,
Having lost their way; and hungry too,
Without grass, water, and trees for shade;
They stood in the burning sun, helplessly lost.

5.7

Searching for the group, he reached them,
Krishna, the lotus-blue eyed, compassionate one,
Swiftly, the Gopas also, to that place, came;
Heat from the sun was like an awesome fire.

5.8

The lotus-eyed Krishna, saw close by,
A spread of brush-land, shady and cool,

Swiftly, the cattle were driven to that place,
But, alas, a fire storm broke out there.

5.9

"Oh, our bodies will be burned by fire,
Krishna, truthfully, you are our salvation",
Seeing the crying folks in great distress,
Lord Krishna smiled and said these words.

5.10

"Be not concerned, cow-herds-men,
Stay with eyes closed, quickly", so said he,
And when they opened their eyes again,
There was neither fire nor the woods in view.

5.11

The brush-woods and the forest fire,
Was an illusion caused by a demon king,
That demon and his magic soon died out,
Know we not - evil acts, to godly men, will fail?

5.12

Along with cows and herdsmen, Krishna,
Stayed in the woods, on Yamuna's shores;
Where, peacock feathers, Asoka, Kadamba trees,
Are found - and passed the warm summer days.

5.13

In the caves of Govardhana mount,
The noble Govinda, Rama and their friends,
The many heavy rainy seasonal days,
In happiness and joy they spent.

5.14

When the months after the rains arrived,
All was clear and the moon shone bright,
The blue lily and the lotus blossomed forth,
Sons of Nanda and their friends enjoyed.

5.15

Cupid like Krishna, went to Nanda's home,
Paid homage to Nanda and held his lotus feet,
Having heard about the good deeds of Krishna,
The Gopa maiden became passionately in love.

5.16

With a hue like that of dark rain clouds,
And peacock feathers in his tuft of hair,
Curly fringes; below that those crafty stares,
Krishna's form was delightful to behold.

5.17

Within his beauteous chest Lakshmi resides,
He wears Srivatsa, Kaustubha, and garlands,

And the golden waist-band to tie his yellow robe,
The form of Vaasudeva was indeed sublime.

5.18

Jewel studded bracelets adorned his arms,
And jingling anklets were on his feet,
Melodious tunes from his flute; and seeing,
Krishna thus, maiden's hearts were wrenched.

5.19

When Krishna went to graze the cattle,
The beautiful women were saddened by it,
Watching the way Krishna would return,
They would longingly wait during dusk.

5.20

To hear tunes like nectar from his flute,
They would forget all, but to hear him play,
And those lotus-eyed beauties, in many words,
They praised the qualities of Krishna's love.

5.21

Once, Gopi maidens, with undue passion,
Wanting to marry the handsome Gopala,
With great inner conviction and faith,
They proceeded to the shores of Yamuna.

5.22

They made with sand, a graceful icon,
Of Parvati, consort of Cupid's Slayer,
Honouring with flowers, water and food,
They worshiped the idol faithfully.

5.23

Praying in mind, with body and words, too,
At the sublime feet of Mukunda,
Then, praying at the feet of the goddess' idol,
The maidens sought freedom from woes.

5.24

Thus they worshipped for a month or more,
And gained the blessings of the goddess,
With the rituals over, and to take a bath,
They entered the pure waters of Yamuna.

5.25

The ladies placed their clothing on the shore,
And when they entered the waters to play,
Then, Vasudeva's son approached,
Stole their clothes and climbed upon a tree.

5.26

Hearing the famed, sublime tunes of the flute,
And on looking, they found Krishna close by,

With modesty, the moon faced ladies stood;
With pride, thinking he is the lord of my heart.

5.27

"Give us our clothes, oh Lord", they asked,
"Yes, if you come and stand in reverence;
Standing with folded hands and begs for them"
So he said, the lotus-eyed-one, smilingly.

5.28

Bashfully, they stood in front of the lord,
Those beautiful maiden, with folded hands,
Then, Krishna gave them their clothes,
And smilingly, said to them, thus:

5.29

"That what you desire I will grant you;
Oh, ladies! There is no lack of love to follow,
There will be many more nights to come,
And we will frolic near Kalindi, in moon light".

5.30

Hearing these words of Govinda,
The beautiful damsels were in ecstasy,
Slowly, they went to their abodes;
Krishna too, to his home, returned.

5.31

Later, they traveled to some far off woods,
The youngsters, with their cattle, too,
But, Krishna noticed, that not having,
Much to eat caused the boys to fatigue.

5.32

Krishna told the boys to go for food,
To the home of a Brahmin; expert at charity,
Hearing this, the hungry boys went,
And they sat ready to receive some food.

5.33

Quickly, the master of the house, informed,
There is naught to give and sent them off,
But, soon after, on Krishna's advice - the boys,
Returned and sought alms from the ladies.

5.34

Then, the chaste Brahmin ladies,
Made rice, dishes, curds, sugar, sweets,
And with due reverence to Krishna,
They waited, patiently, to meet him.

5.35

In defiance of their husbands who cried,
Angrily, "Stop, do not give them food",

Their wives, with great devotion, stood,
At Krishna's feet, and gave them food.

5.36

A chaste lady, obeyed her husband's wish,
To stay far away from the rest of the group,
Behold, what wonder: she cast her soul from,
Her body, and gained union with the Lord.

5.37

At that time, the masters of the sacrifice,
Gained inner understanding of the events;
Blessing the fair ladies and the Brahmins,
Krishna returned to his place with happiness.

5.38

At that time, the capable Nandagopa,
Decided to perform a sacrifice for Indra,
Then the Lord, being there, asked mildly,
What is the purpose of staring this ritual?

5.39

Nanada said: "All the good things we have,
We owe to the blessings of Indra, no less,
Thus, the timely rain that falls on earth,
And all the bounties thereof are due to him".

5.40

Considering it is Indra who provides,
Grass and water for the cows; we deem him,
To be the supreme god, and thusly,
We perform this sacrifice hastily, my son".

5.41

The lotus eyed one gently replied:
"It is not Indra, father, the provider of rain,
But, an unforeseen force is the real cause,
And even Indra is subject to its effect.

5.42

Govardhana mountain is the esteemed cause,
Father, believe the growth in cows is due to it,
And, forget not that Brahmins grant happiness,
It is true that this way one finds the objective.

5.43

Hark, Brahmins! Cause this world to prosper,
Food be given to them, and gifts too,
Give unto Govardhana and the Brahmins,
Start now a sacrifice in their favour".

5.44

Hearing these words of the son of Vasudeva,
The Nanda clan was overcome with joy,

After worshipping the mountain and Brahmins,
A great sacrifice was gradually prepared.

5.45

In the mountain's form, he ate the offered food,
To reduce Indra's pride, Govinda,
Took the offered food kept aside for Indra,
And he gave it to the mountain and the priests.

5.46

Indra's mind was steeped in rage,
His thousand eyes looked askance,
He caused torrential rain to fall;
He tried to end the sacrifice, by flood.

5.47

Overcome with fury, he brought on,
The rain clouds that causes floods,
It began to rain as great thunder roared,
With much joy peacocks began to dance.

5.48

The hail rained down copiously,
It fell on the body like death itself,
The cows unable to bear the heavy fall,
They gathered around the feet of Acyuta.

5.49

Then, Govinda, to protect the cows,
Picked Govardhana Mountain by his hands,
And, the sublime, remover of all worldly woes,
He raised it high, and held it as an umbrella.

5.50

The Gopa maidens with great devotion,
Praised Gopala and stayed there with joy,
Holding the mountain in his right hand,
He stroked the bovines gently with his left.

5.51

He stood, for seven days, holding the hill,
As Vishnu, the frequent destroyer of pride,
Thus, when Indra lost his haughtiness,
He gladly halted the torrential rain.

5.52

Krishna, placed down the hill and went home,
And proceeded to his amorous plays,
Indra and his group of divine maids,
They bowed low to the brother of Rama.

5.53

From thence he came to be called Govinda,
A name that adorns the speech of populace,

Then, the divine cow, Kamadhenu,
Came and anointed Krishna with holy milk.

5.54

Iravata, holding one thousand jars,
Of the pure waters of heavenly Ganga,
Began to shower over the head of Narayana,
And all the fourteen worlds glowed with joy.

5.55

Hearing these unusual stories of merit;
Seeing the gods from heaven worship,
Nanda and his clan knew Krishna's truth,
But, held it back; continuing normal life.

5.56

Once, when Vasudeva was bathing in Kalindi,
He was captured by the forces of Varuna,
Acyuta, four-armed, went into the depths,
And he gladly brought his father back.

5.57

To favour the wishes of the Gopa damsels,
Once, Krishna went, after sunset,
To stand at the moon-lit shores of Yamuna,
And he played melodious tunes on his flute.

5.58

Hearing the sublime tunes from his flute,
Gopi damsels were hit by Cupid's darts,
Caring not for self, wealth, and others,
With hope, they hastened, to Yamuna's banks.

5.59

One maiden wore heavy jewelry in places,
While another, in hurry, wore no gold,
Another Gopi, on her way and in haste,
She dropped her silken upper garment off.

5.60

Ignoring their husbands and children,
The milk-maids hastened to Krishna;
Under the spell of Cupid's sharp darts,
Will a maiden pay heed to anything else?

5.61

Past woods, ravines, deep rivers and canals,
They ran to reach their beloved by dusk,
These stories of the wide-eyed maidens run,
Heavenly musicians sing about, to this day.

5.62

Those infatuated beauties that came to him,
The dark-skinned lord blessed them well,

To probe the feelings of these lovely maids,
The lord spoke of the path of righteousness.

5.63

"Having given up your homes and wealth;
You pretty ladies visit here most honorable?
Do not chaste women consider as true,
Their husbands are the only true god to know?

5.64

Freedom of thought is not a woman's choice,
And also to desire some one else in mind,
Is it not truly wanting for us to mete,
Peace in after life, by doing acts today?

5.65

It is ordained that women not walk alone,
If they be out past day light hours,
It is not proper to walk through woods,
This, all married women should know in full.

5.66

Tarry no longer, then, but return,
To your husbands and serve them well",
When the Gopis heard Krishna's words,
The damsels, in distress, replied thus:

5.67

"Like unto Cupid in looks, oh kindly lord,
Refrain from words that are not to taste,
Bearing the searing hot arrows of Cupid,
Beautiful-eyed women are in flames.

5.68

Woe! Oh Lord, we are saddened to depart;
What once we cherished we now abstain,
When we, sandal paste or moon glow, touch,
They seem to sear – most honestly.

5.69

The drone of bees from within the flowers,
Droplets of honey dew on lotus blooms,
Hearing the chirping of nightingale chicks,
These things are pleasant to us - no more.

5.70

When the gentle hill breeze blows Kadamba,
Jasmine and flower juice scents on our skin,
It burns like love-viper's venom – Oh Krishna,
Save us, you who have a moon-like face.

5.71

You have the appearance and luster,
Of Cupid, and his charm to attract,

Grant us kindly what we seek of you,
Need you speak such unsavoury words?

5.72

Hearing the pleading words of the damsels,
Quickly did Krishna, with much kindness,
And with mind-yielding sweet words,
He began to play with the moon-faced dames.

5.73

Like unto the sublime moon in shine,
Skillful in the art of amorous plays -
The god of gods, eulogized by,
The two sages Vyasa and Narada -
With a smile on his lotus like face,
The Lord of infinite beatitude,
The lotus-eyed god began the games,
When crowded by the graceful maids.

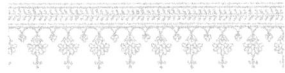

dance of love

6.1

By the shores Kalindi, with the damsels,
Krishna, began to dance exquisitely,
In rhythm to the music of the flute,
And the instrumental to the raga beats.

6.2

The erotic maiden began to dance,
With songs to the tune of the veena,
Wearing ornaments fitting to their sleeves,
They looked beautiful in their attire.

6.3

Though to many Gopis, like Radha,
Krishna was the prime attraction,
But, assuming multiple forms,
He paired with many damsels there.

6.4

Those pot-like breasts on Gopis's chests,
Krishna, sought, intimately to embrace;
Sublimely, he kissed to taste the nectar,
That made for Cupid's festive mood.

6.5

Their pink lips were reddened by the chew,
Of beetle-leaf and nuts and so blossomed;
Krishna, with excessive acts of love,
Gratified them all, with amorous moves.

6.6

In that land, permeated with the scent,
Of musk, sandal paste and saffron dust,
The high breasted women were embraced,
And, besides, acts of free indiscretion began.

6.7

Then to see the games of love in play,
The demigods, the celestials, divine musicians,
Heavenly maids, the Moon, Gods, Narada,
And more came and assembled in the sky.

6.8

Then, heavenly gods, poured copiously,
Celestial flowers on Krishna's body,

Along side that, the heavenly nymphs,
Also began to dance to different tunes.

6.9

Each maiden thought that,
"No one is as fortunate as I am",
"No one dear to Krishna as I am",
"I am surely the most fortunate".

6.10

This prince glances not at other maids:
Hence my life is rich; mine is a festival,
My desires have come to be fulfilled;
With a perfect man as this, my life is full.

6.11

I am the gratifying one; I am the fortunate;
I am beautiful; I am endeared; I am pretty;
I have virtue; I am the most acceptable;
So each felt convinced - those pretty maiden.

6.12

"Nymphs like Urvashi can match me not,
Then, can mere mortals compete with me?
Krishna, can love none; only me",
So, each Gopi thought, with much pride.

6.13

In order to thwart the growing pride,
In the minds of the cow-maidens,
The great spirit of the cosmos,
Krishna, with coy Radha, vanished from the site.

6.14

Then, the damsel crowd cried with grief,
Wandering the entire forest in search,
"No, Krishna, do not cheat us,
What did we maiden do to earn this?

6.15

Oh lord of immense kindness; pay heed,
Cow-herd women have none but you to seek,
Why are you so unkind, Oh Krishna?
What can you do to relieve our sadness?

6.16

Sad! We eschewed people and wealth,
Now, we are laughed at by the entire world,
We are on the road of misery,
Oh Lord Krishna, you fooled the damsels.

6.17

What qualities does Radha have over us?
Yet, now you choose to live with her,

Never did we think of your cunning ways,
That got us to this sorrow and ill repute.

6.18

Is it proper that you, should play,
Such improper deception on us, oh lord?
The great sages say, that in this world,
You remove the misery of the miserable.

6.19

You are as soothing as the cool moon,
Why are you now the source of misery?
We have no way to think, oh Krishna,
Why we burn like embers in this misery?

6.20

You have in the past deceived the maids,
Now, we learn for certain that this is so,
In the past when a woman with big breasts,
Came to give you milk, you killed her fast.

6.21

I have no grief if you kill me now,
I can merge again with your divine feet,
What was done is the most egregious,
Having rejected me you live secretly".

6.22

Such words were thus addressed,
Yet, their sadness saw no slack from him,
Later wandering in the woods,
They talked to the trees, their plight.

6.23

"Tell me kindly, oh, sweet mango tree,
Seen you, the like of a handsome youth?
Had you seen him you too will conclude,
He is surely equal to the God of Love".

6.24

"Jasmine flower, give us news of him,
So that our minds may in peace recline,
There is no joy in us – if God rejects -
Then fate is same, to all, oh, jasmine flower"!

6.25

"Hear our sorrow, oh, Asoka tree,
Krishna is the full moon to the world,
Sigh! He has abandoned the maids,
And lives secluded in Radha's arms".

6.26

"Hear this, oh, shaky palash tree,
You too may feel sadness in your mind,

Treating us as common folks, the noble one,
He quickly vanished from our midst".

6.27

"Give us, oh, amaranth bush, all details,
If Krishna had perchance passed by you,
Having left the good grace of our company,
Is he hiding in the forest; far from us?"

6.28

"In haste we speak, oh jasmine flower,
Krishna has vanquished us, most sadly,
Having gathered us together, he has left,
We say this to remind - our lives are lost".

6.29

"Hear this, hear this, oh little hen-bird,
Do not hesitate to speak openly to us,
Has our amorous Krishna turned so cruel?
He was the master of the games of love.

6.30

Black cloudy hair, adorned with feathers;
Body shining in color like Asoka buds;
With long blue eyes, and pleasant smile,
These attributes of Vishnu are on him seen".

6.31

"Oh honey bee, are you certain that,
You have not seen the form of Krishna, yet?
For, had you seen the sweet lotus look of his,
You will never leave the proximity of his face".

6.32

"Sing the glory, oh nightingales,
Of the sweet tunes of his sublime flute,
Know that it is ambrosia to the ear,
Surely, only the lucky have heard it played".

6.33

"Oh, prancing pea-cocks - should you see,
The singing Lord Krishna,
The pride of your bright neck will fade,
And jealousy will reign in your mind"

6.34

"He is the man engrossed in erotic love,
His sublime smile bespeaks his character,
Oh swan! Have you seen Radha's lover today?
If not, note the features to know him by.

6.35

On his chest is the glorious Kaustubha gem,
And also the distinct mark called Srivatsa,

Moreover, Govinda has the robe of yellow silk,
And he is fond of herds of cows".

6.36

Come, come, oh wild elephant,
Have you seen Govinda in hither woods?
The beauty of his graceful walk,
Will make you feel embarrassed".

6.37

While the Gopi maids were so distraught,
And walked about with sorrow,
They saw Radha, by Krishna rejected,
She came swiftly to join them.

6.38

She had roamed the woods, despondent,
She had questioned beasts, birds and plants,
She had, weeping, shed copious tears,
She had been wounded by Cupid's shafts.

6.39

Lord Krishna, knowing the plight,
Of the sorrow filled Gopi maidens,
Kindness filled the heart of the lord,
And he appeared quickly in their midst.

6.40

Due lack of words, its hard to describe,
The joy and pleasure the maidens felt,
Krishna, began to play with the maids,
More than he previously engaged.

6.41

The group of sorrow-filled Gopi women,
Felt relieved by the divine gaze of Krishna,
Like rain from dark-blue clouds that drench,
The dryness caused by the burning sun.

6.42

Then, a maiden with high amorous want,
And with other maidens watching,
Caught the hands of her beloved lover,
And on her breasts she pressed.

6.43

Another maid pressed her raised breasts,
Against the garlanded chest of Krishna,
And with sexual desire was engulfed,
She united with him in exotic ecstasy.

6.44

Another woman, entrapped by desire,
With sweat-beads garlanding her breasts,

Placed the lotus-like feet of Krishna,
The Lord worshipped in the Vedas, on her lap.

6.45

Krishna, who looked like Cupid,
Lay on a bed prepared of flowers,
And when he lay down there,
The Gopi maiden came close to him.

6.46

Swiftly, a gem like woman of the clan,
Placed, on her lap, Krishna's hair,
That wafted scent like coral-tree bloom,
And, she gently stroked her nails through.

6.47

A maiden who dearly adored Krishna,
Held his feet in her lotus like hands,
Dust off Krishna's feet; only the lucky get,
She was most fortunate to gather, fast.

6.48

Another maiden sitting close by,
With a fan in her hand; ready to attend,
Watching the blissful face of Krishna,
She began to fan his body, softly.

6.49

One stately maiden, brought forth,
A sandal scent dispenser and stood by,
And then with her tender hands,
She sprayed droplets on Krishna's form.

6.50

One maiden, deep in sexual passion,
Began erotic dances, that would awe,
Even the nymphs, and to seek as an offering,
Union with Krishna, who adores the maids.

6.51

A maiden, sulking due to lack of love,
With an angry face, sat away,
Not hearing the taunts of her mates -
Tears flowing from her lotus like face.

6.52

One woman, sitting close by, began to talk,
Repeatedly, of the sorrows of separation:
"If you discard me for another woman,
Then, you will be the cause my demise".

6.53

A Gopi stitching a garland with white lilies,
Tied the plaited flowers on Krishna's feet,

"You must not make an effort even to take,
A single step" - so said she to her lord!

6.54

This way, Krishna, with the Gopi maids,
Enjoyed many types of amorous plays,
Thereafter, the night began to cease,
And the nectarine moon to dip.

6.55

The brightness of the stars began to fade,
Some where, far, cocks began to crow,
Cupid's flowery bow was now less taut,
Soon after, the East began to glow.

6.56

Chakrakava hen was joined by her mate,
Darkness began to lighten in the woods,
The lotus flowers began to bloom,
Morning chorus songs were heard aloud.

6.57

At that time, over the eastern mount,
The solar orb glowed, after the dawn,
Soon after, Krishna left his berth,
And with him, the damsels left for home.

6.58

One day, to attend the a jubilant festival,
At the temple of Ambika in the city,
And with all his clan, along with him,
Krishna proceeded to go, with joy.

6.59

At that time, Nanda was bitten,
By a big snake feared by men,
But, Krishna swiftly severed the snake,
And it took the form of a lovely maid.

6.60

"You of the discus, conch and lotus,
I am Sudarshana, an aerial spirit,
By your kind pardon my curse is off,
And I am now free".

6.61

Having said so, the divine spirit faded,
After liberation the noble one rejoiced,
The cow-herdsmen also went their way,
To their separate homes and happily lived.

6.62

Once, the lotus-eyed Krishna, the Gopis,
And Balarama, went to the woods,

There they saw a slave of Kubera,
Shamkhachooda filled with erotic desires.

6.63

When he tried to molest the women,
Krishna quickly blocked his move,
And slaying him he plucked the jewel,
Off his head, and gave to Balarama to keep.

6.64

A cruel demon, named Anishta,
By magic, took the form of a bull,
Having entered the cow-pen,
It began to frolic in many ways.

6.65

The bull which was playing such pranks,
Was killed there by Lord Krishna,
Then the young and old Gopas,
Lost their fears and became happy.

6.66

When, that pompous Asura named Kesi,
Assuming the form of a horse,
Entered Ambadi to cause chaos,
Then, Krishna, lifting him quickly by his legs,

Smashed him to the ground and killed him,
It was then that Krishna, gained,
The name, Keshava – he who killed Kesi,
That beauteous name, he thus acquired.

6.67

Vyoma, son of an Asura, named Maya,
Deceived the Gopas and their cattle,
And held them in a cave, till Krishna,
Having killed him brought peace to the land.

6.68

Thus having killed the evil ones,
He brought rectitude to Gopa's land,
Giver of delight; residing in good men,
May he - sublime son of Nanda - give us joy!

death of kamsa

7.1

Narada, white as the autumn cloud,
The exalted leader among the saints,
Reached the abode of the King of Bhoja,
Kamsa: The crest jewel of fearless kings.

7.2

Kamsa, with respect, met the saint,
Wetted the sage's face and feet,
And placed him on a seat, with humility,
Then, the Brahmin Narada said these words:

7.3

"You are the primary ruler of the world,
And with your awesome strength,
You have conquered the three realms too,
Oh, foremost of wisest men!

7.4

The glory of your fame has flown,
And cast such brightness o'er lands,
Even Siva cannot find, by your shine,
The crystal mount, Kailasa, where he lives.

7.5

If the extent of your glory is sought,
Oh, King of Bhoja; it is endless!
Even the divine maidens of the gods,
Who play in the garden of heaven, praise thee.

7.6

It is indeed sad to note,
That you have only one enemy,
Why does the conqueror the worlds,
Find it impossible to win over this one?

7.7

You have but only one enemy,
And it is rather sad perhaps to deem,
That one who has won the three realms,
Find not the strength to crush this one?

7.8

One named Krishna,
Is well known in the Yadava clan,

His brother, Rama, by name,
In body hue and shade is white.

7.9

Your emissaries like, Putana,
Krishna has sent to the realm of the dead,
They who wear the yellow and blue robes,
Indeed are they the sons of Vasudeva.

7.10

Krishna, is the son of Devaki,
He grants victory to the Devas,
Rama, is the son of Rohini,
By his looks, he is like unto Cupid".

7.11

Hearing such words of the saint,
The king became elevated with anger,
As Kamsa was to send the order to destroy,
The family of Vasudeva, Narada, further, spoke:

7.12

"You are not ruling as a king,
To perform such horrific deeds,
Do not be cruel": said the sage;
Thusly, he talked him off the wrong path.

7.13

Slowly, Sage Narada went away,
To his abode in the Land of Truth,
The cruel Kamsa soon beckoned,
Akrura and such measured words he said:

7.14

"Oh, son of Gandini; of good breeding,
Go to the abode of Nandagopa,
And after telling him these proper words,
Return, today, without delay.

7.15

"Rama and Krishna, must come, soon,
To my own city, for we wish, in course,
To conduct a Sacrifice of the Bow,
That is to serve my brave warriors.

7.16

I need to see my children,
Do not tarry, but go forth,
Bring the two boys together, to me,
Oh, noble-man; do this without delay".

7.17

So ordered, the Son of Gandini, went forth,
Swiftly, following the commands given,

Thinking in mind, how fortunate,
It was to see the face of Krishna, again?

7.18

Riding on the chariot, swiftly,
Contemplating on the feet of Krishna,
He rode over mountains and forests,
And saw the shaded woods by the Yamuna.

7.19

Picking some dust from the foot print,
Of Krishna, he placed it on his head,
And repeating the name of Krishna,
That reduces woe; he gently prayed aloud.

7.20

By about evening, he reached,
The residence of Nandagopa,
There he quickly saw, Krishna,
Standing with full of grace and mirth.

7.21

Akrura saw, Krishna, dark as clouds,
Pick a milk jar by his lotus hands,
And as he drank the full content,
He enjoyed other playful games too.

7.22

Wearing a yellow dress with a girdle,
And a pea-feather in his bundled hair,
With pretty eyes and in colour as dark clouds,
Akrura saw that youthful form.

7.23

Approaching, Rama and Krishna,
Having such sublime characteristics,
The noble-man, stood with folded hands,
And the Son of Nanda addressed him thus:

7.24

"Oh, Son of Gandini, how fare you?
Note, you're coming pleases me well,
It has always pained me in my heart,
You and others were not here before".

7.25

Krishna, having said only these words,
Hugged the mild-mannered one, Akrura,
Embraced by Krishna,
Akrura gained everlasting joy and bliss.

7.26

Having partaken food at night,
Akrura stayed at a resplendent house,

The King of Bhoja's entire call,
Krishna heard with deep attention.

7.27

Slowly, Krishna replied, thus:
"Kamsa's orders are fine indeed,
It is good that the king begins,
To do the Ritual of the Bow, as planned.

7.28

My uncle, the great ruler,
Has with sweetness sent for Your Honour,
Can this be a deceitful act?
Nobel Sir, pray tell me your belief?

7.29

Tomorrow morning we will journey,
I want to walk there, every where,
Hear - I want to see the merriment,
That comes with the Offering to the Bow.

7.30

The treachery that is established,
In my uncle's heart, will not affect me,
Do not be concerned or anxious,
Harbour no fear in mind, my friend".

7.31

Krishna, having spoken thus,
Retired to bed and so too his friend,
And at the time when the sun rose,
He climbed into the chariot with Rama, too.

7.32

Hearing of the travels of the Gopa youths,
The Gopi maidens became sad,
Those who were staying in their homes,
They began to fault Akrura for their loss.

7.33

"Came here a cruel rouge lately,
So, I heard the hard facts, companions!
Who is he to have done such deeds?
For what merit is that cruel man involved?

7.34

"Cruel" is the name he bears, though a fool,
Gave him a name opposite in nature,
Perhaps, his name suggests that,
There is no one crueler than him.

7.35

Krishna, the darling of the maidens,
Has been made a captive now,

He it was who bade Krishna to the cart,
Only he will find that to his choice.

7.36

If I am separated from Krishna,
I will have no desire to live,
Rather than this worthless life,
I would think of drinking poison.

7.37

If we are parted from his countenance,
The virtue of life will soon be worthless,
Cupid dart your arrows to hit our hearts;
By striking that vital organ we may die!

7.38

To remove the distress by which,
Those beautiful maidens were living,
Krishna, with kindness, sent his friend,
Akrura, and asked him to comfort them.

7.39

Hearing the soft words of Gandini's son,
The turmoil in Gopis hearts were lost,
And with many Gopa friends in tow,
Krishna set to travel by chariot.

7.40

Krishna with Rama and other Gopas,
With Akrura as the charioteer,
Came to Kalindi River; daughter of the Sun,
And came to its wind swept shores.

7.41

Akrura, dipped in the waters,
Before he rose an awesome sight beheld,
Vishnu, supine on Ananta,
He saw with great joy in the waters.

7.42

"Oh, Krishna, how wonderful indeed,
I saw the form of Vishnu in the waters,
Your state is beyond compare,
You of the cosmic form, I bow to thee"!

7.43

Krishna - who grants blessings,
To those who follow such devotees,
And sing his praise with clarity,
And devotion - reached Mathura.

7.44

That night he spent at Akrura's abode,
The lord of the world enjoyed his stay,

The next day, early in the morning,
That noble lord continued the journey.

7.45

On the royal causeway he walked,
Without caution but with guile,
Then with a bundle of clothes,
A washer man came up to Krishna.

7.46

Saying he had no clothes, Krishna,
Extended his hands seeking some clothes,
Abruptly, the washer man became angry,
And he replied in a course language.

7.47

"If you talk not knowing what you say,
You may then be beaten - you fool!
This clothes bundle belongs to the king,
Shameless one – harm may come to you!"

7.48

So saying, that servant of the king,
Began to leave the scene in anger,
But, Krishna plucked the bundle of robes,
And he quickly decapitated the washer-man.

7.49

The washer man was granted salvation,
And without concern Krishna proceeded,
He granted his blessings to a flower vendor,
When, the vendor gave him a splendid garland.

7.50

In front of the lotus eyed one,
Came a crippled girl,
The protector of the worlds, quickly,
Held her hand and cured her of her stoop.

7.51

She gave to the lotus-eyed lord,
Sandal-wood scented saffron dust,
Then struck by the arrows of Cupid,
That pretty maiden's heart was lured.

7.52

"Oh, Cupid-like Krishna,
Relieve my love laden wants,
I am most desirous of that need":
So, said the lovely maiden; bowing down.

7.53

"Oh, Parrot like Beauty, be patient,
All your sorrow will soon be over,

Well within some four or five days,
I will return to your side": he said.

7.54

With Balarama and the Gopas in tow,
Krishna, went to the palace without delay,
It seemed when seeing his sublime form,
That his garland was made of lover's glances.

7.55

Bravely, he entered the pavilion of the bow,
And picked up the bow with his hands,
Swiftly, he pulled the bow to bend,
Then, he-who-rides-the-eagle broke the bow.

7.56

Those, many, many guardians of the bow,
Becoming angry, approached to kill,
But, Krishna picked the broken bow pieces,
And beat that multitude and killed them.

7.57

Hearing the sound of the breaking bow,
All eight quarters of the world trembled,
Kamsa trembled and fell to the ground,
The gods in heaven rejoiced greatly.

7.58

Krishna walked two miles in length,
And saw the entire city of Mathura,
It kindled in him some small excitement,
To see the location, where he was born,

7.59

The market, buildings like made of gems,
Town-gate, turrets and fine palaces,
The armory and the king's mansion,
All these the Gopa clan, walked to see.

7.60

Then, Krishna, unknown to others,
Went to his parent's abode,
He reverently mentioned all the news,
Their sorrow removed, he left accordingly.

7.61

Sons of Nanda - Krishna and Rama,
Wandered in the city, till dusk,
They walked with others of the Gopa clan,
And at night-fall they rested in a house.

7.62

Then, Kamsa, the King of the Worlds,
Climbed the high palace, to be seated,

The boxers with their war-drums,
Stood there ready to do battle,
Other kings of kinship, sat on thrones,
And the mahouts placed a raging,
Elephant, that was in rut, at the palace gate.

7.63

Krishna, resplendent in the heavy garland,
Received from the boy, and other ornaments,
With the Gopas and Balarama, too,
Prepared to destroy the enemy;
And they saw, standing at the gate,
The angry, elephant in rut,
Kuvalayapeeda, and its wicked mount;
Both were killed by Krishna, swiftly.

7.64

One was the boxer, Chanura,
And the other was named Mushtaka,
These fools, shaking the ground,
Quickly began to ready for the fight,
At that time, Krishna and Balarama,
Joined to return the fight,
The powerful boxing bout, sounding loud,
It was heard all around.

7.65

The assailant, Chanura, was dispatched,
To Yama's abode, by Krishna's blows,
The King of Bhoja's arrogance fell,
When Rama destroyed Mushtaka, as well,
Their family members cried;
And the wicked leaders fled with fear,
When, with that nectar like smile,
Krishna's music resonated from his flute.

7.66

Krishna saw, up above,
The King of Bhoja in great anxiety,
Krishna, jumped leaping, brilliantly,
To the balcony and with much anger,
Grasping the deceitful king by the neck,
He threw him down on the floor,
And cut his throat with the sword;
He stood on Kamsas's chest, unruffled.

7.67

The splendor that was heightened in the king,
Merged with the luster in Krishna's form,
Eight brothers of Kamsa were also killed,
The gods poured flowers on this worthy state.

7.68

He humbly paid respects to his parents,

And embraced them tightly on the cheek,
Then the great devotee, the wise Udhava,
He paid obeisance to Krishna with great joy.

7.69

Ugrasena, who can handle all stately tasks,
Was swiftly ordained king of the land,
To care for the welfare of the people,
Krishna stayed in Mathura, for a long time.

rukmini's wedding

8.1

Once, dutifully and with one mind,
Rama and Krishna prepared to seek higher learning.

8.2

To Saint Sandeepani they went, with due respect,
And they learned all sacred texts by his tutoring.

8.3

Having learned all the scholarship fast and fully,
They considered what tuition gift to give him kindly?

8.4

At the teachers request they went to Varuna's realm,
To seek the teacher's son who was drowned in a lake.

8.5

Krishna, killed Panjajanam and took his conch,
Panchajanyam,
Then they went to the land of Yama to free the teacher's
son.

8.6

Having given the boy as a gift for tuition services rendered,
They were blessed by the saint and to Mathura, returned.

8.7

At one time, Krishna, the embodiment of kindness,
The trusted Udhava to the land of the Gopas, he sent.

8.8

In talks, Udhava, removed the Gopi's anguish,
And after that he returned to Krishna.

8.9

Krishna, spent the night, in a delightful way, at the home,
Of the perfume selling maiden whom he had made
beautiful.

8.10

A son was born to the couple following that romance,
That boy named, Upashloka, became famous world-wide.

8.11

One day, Krishna, the wielder of the discus,
With Udhava went to meet Akrura, his beloved friend.

8.12

At that time, hearing of the Pandavas,
He sent Akrura to find of their whereabouts.

8.13

King of Magadha, was angry at Kamsa's death,
Thus, the mighty Jarasandha came to battle.

8.14

He surrounded the city of Mathura, with a mighty army,
At which time, Krishna too prepared to battle.

8.15

Indra had given two chariots of grandeur,
Balarama mounted one and Krishna the other.

8.16

Rama and Krishna, with an army of brave soldiers,
Began a counter attack, and Jarasandha fled.

8.17

Balarama caught Jarasandha and prepared to kill him,
But, Krishna intervened and let him go.

8.18

The King of Magadha attacked again and again,
And Krishna reprieved him, repeatedly.

8.19

Three and three times three, hundred army corps,
Of Magadha, were destroyed by Krishna in battle.

8.20

During the eighteenth time of the cruel king's attacks,
He came with Yavana king; thousand, thousands more.

8.21

When Krishna heard of the advent of the Yavana army,
He decided to build his own abode, Dwaraka, north in the
sea.

8.22

That city, by the divine architect, Vishvakarma, built,
To Krishna's need - the most splendid in the world.

8.23

Many subjects living in Mathura,
Krishna took them to live in Dwaraka city.

8.24

Krishna himself traveled to meet the Yavana directly,
Pretending to be afraid, he ran into the woods.

8.25

The Yavana ran behind the fleeing Krishna,
Playfully, Krishna hid inside a cave close by.

8.26

When he searched for Krishna in the woods,
The Yavana saw King Mucukunda sleeping in a corner,

8.27

He stomped on Mucukunda thinking he was Krishna,
And in turn the Yavana was quickly burned to ashes.

8.28

Waking from sleep, he saw the blissful form of Vishnu,
Emerging from the hillside, and standing besides him.

8.29

His four hands held, conch, discuss, mace and the lotus,
He stood resplendent with the holy mark, gem and garland.

8.30

Seeing the Cosmic Form, Muchukunda, worshipped him
thus:
"Praise to thee, oh Lord of Vaikunda; Cause of the World.

8.31

I am the scion of Ikasku line of kings, oh Lord of Lakshmi,
But, I find protecting and punishing beyond my own desire.

8.32

In that state I had come to spend countless days, oh Lord,
I have no further interest in sons, friends or even wives.

8.33

I must gain your blessing to wipe out my misery,
I prostrate at your feet, as Sankara and others do too.

8.34

He gains salvation, who is truly devoted to you,
Bowing to your feet may devotion rise within me.

8.35

Enough, if you bless that I gain the same as your devotees,
By remembering your feet, my sins will surely go away.

8.36

Krishna gave Muchukunda the devotion to gain salvation,
Then he moved to Mathura to destroy Yavana's army.

8.37

King of Magadha returned to battle once more,
But, Krishna feigned defeat; retreated; giving him victory.

8.38

Krishna returned to Dwaraka and lived contentedly,
Nandagopa and his clan also came to live there happily.

8.39

At this time, Balarama married a maiden,
Her name was Revati, the daughter of Revata.

8.40

Bhishmaka, King of Vidarbha, feared by his enemies,
He began to make preparations for his daughter's wedding.

8.41

The king consented to give his lotus-eyed daughter Rukmini,
To Shishupala, as insisted by his son named Rukmi.

8.42

When she heard she was betrothed to the King of Chedi,
That virgin, who loved Krishna, was overcome with grief.

8.43

Rukmini, in great secrecy, directed a Brahmin,
To visit and return quickly from Krishna's abode.

8.44

The Brahmin started on the journey to Dwaraka City,
And he delivered the message to Krishna without delay.

8.45

"Lord Krishna; Oh, Govinda, listen to my words, earnestly,
I bring this message from Rukmini, daughter of King
Bhishmaka.

8.46

'I bow to you, who are like Indra, Overall Guide, Sea of
Kindness,
I have a request of thee - kindly do not reject my plea.

8.47

In hue, like the dark clouds; beloved of damsels,
Merciful lord, I seek refuge at your red lotus colored feet.

8.48

Right now, my father, mother, brothers and friends,
They jointly engage in advancing events against my wish.

8.49

My family members are intently involved,
They plan to give me away to the evil Sishupala.

8.50

For me, Krishna, it is far better to die,
Rather than marry that cruel and arrogant king!

8.51

Kind hearted lord, kindly come and carry me off,
With such happy ending, my family will be overjoyed

8.52

Life-birth, wealth, also, soul and body too,
Mother and father, all that, at your feet I lay.

8.53

You carry me away; before the time of marriage,
Oh, Great Lord, I bow to thee': So said Rukmini.

8.54

'If I gain not the pleasure of being united with you,
Then, I will give up my life today': So said Rukmini.

8.55

'Protect me and save my life, lord who is fathomless,
I pay homage at your feet': So said Rukmini".

8.56

To the Brahmin who spoke thus,
Krishna said: "Go forth, and I will follow you".

8.57

"Oh, Brahmin, having heard the many virtues of Rukmini,
I too am tormented by love, and I am weakened thereby.

8.58

In my mind resides the memory of that beautiful maiden,
Swiftly and without delay, I will come and carry her away".

8.59

Having said thus, and attired in beautiful clothes,
Krishna climbed into his chariot, without Balarama.

8.60

With a calm demeanor and the emblem of Garuda on his flag,
Krishna proceeded to Kundina City; after the Brahmin had left.

8.61

The Brahmin went immediately to meet the royal maiden,
He conveyed Krishna's words to her and swiftly consoled her.

8.62

Then, the great and powerful Balarama,
Hearing of Krishna's venture proceeded to Vidarbha too.

8.63

When these two honourable persons reached the city,
Bhishmaka received them kindly and sat them on a gem-throne.

8.64

Sishupala and other kings, were in high confusion,
And as a riotous group, they were seated in the throne
room.

8.65

To worship the Goddess, at the famed temple of Durga,
Rukmini, radiantly attired with many jewelry, arrived
gracefully.

8.67

"Whither go thou; most beautiful gem of all damsels",
So saying, Krishna approached Rukmini, gently.

8.68

The brave and noble Krishna, softly held her tender hand,
And lifting her into the chariot drove away.

8.69

"Who is this deceitful man", the kings gathered there asked,
"Who has stolen the pretty princess and taken her by
chariot"?

8.70

"Beat them, you fools; stop them; you kings of the realms,
Pick your arrows and attach to your bows; tarry not."

8.71

That angry group of kings came forward, with battle cries,
Udhava and the Yadava kings fought back and ran them off.

8.72

When Rukmi came brandishing his golden sword,
Krishna prepared to decapitate him.

8.73

"Oh, young warrior, kill not your wife's brother,
Pardon him; disfigure him to shame instead."

8.74

Hearing these forceful words of Balarama,
Krishna cut the hair from Rukmi's head, and freed him.

8.75

In company of Balarama and companions,
And with Rukmini, Krishna went to Dwaraka to live
happily.

8.76

At his abode, Krishna lay on the couch with the beautiful
lady,
The lotus-eyed one reached out and held her soft hands.

8.78

At her companion's cajoling, her shyness lessened daily,
By her husband's gentle lead, she was learning lover's skills.

8.79

She lost her restrain due to shyness; gone was her inner
doubts,
She rejoiced freely with her husband, the most beautiful
Rukmini.

8.80

Jeweled homes, courtyards, gardens, lakes,
Aromatic sandal-wood forests to play in,
Many similar places of sublime nature,
Krishna took the beautiful Rukmini to see.

8.81

They played in the woods; hid in golden boughs;
They slept as beloveds on comfortable couch,
Krishna, who delights in the games of love, rejoiced,
They sojourned for a time, with exceeding joy.

ix

the curse of the jewel

9.1

At that time, living there, close by,
A noble Yadava named Satrajit lived,
By the grace of the Sun God,
He received a gem, shining like the sun.

9.2

Wearing the gem named Syamanthaka,
That brightened the area with its shine,
And as he came by people wrongly thought,
This was, indeed, the Sun God walking.

9.3

"Oh Krishna, the Sun is coming,
So bow down to your feet´- they said,
At that instance, he just glanced casually -
That lotus eyed, Krishna.

9.4

Grasping the situation, Krishna came,
To Satrajit and asked him thus:
"Please give me this valuable gem,
I will pay much wealth for it".

9.5

Hearing these words of Krishna,
The Yadava thought inwardly,
"Even he who has enough to manage,
Has deep desire to acquire greater wealth.

9.6

"Will I give, for free, this jewel?
That I obtained after long penance?
Eight times eight are the units of gold,
This gem gives daily, without fail.

9.7

This gem, obtained after much hardship,
I will not permit one to take from me,
If in haste I give this to some one,
In times of need will there be credit"?

9.8

Thinking so, that greedy fool,
Retreated from there with scorn,

Going to his home with no further thought,
He lived happily with the income, earned.

9.9

Then, that Yadava's brother, Prasena,
Made ready to go on a hunting trip,
And seeking the gem from his elder brother,
He wore it happily around his neck.

9.10

With tribal folks and dogs in tow,
He was setting for a long hunt in the woods,
Then his startled horse ran far away;
And he was separated from the group.

9.11

A savage lion, chanced upon him,
That dwelt deep in the darkest woods,
It struck the youth and killed him too,
And bit the gem and walked away.

9.12

Romping there was a heroic ape,
He struck the lion and killed it soon,
The gem that fell at his feet he picked,
And he went happily to his cave.

9.13

Jambavan, the ape, gave the jewel,
To his son who came closely by,
He playfully bit the gem;
He began sporting with it like a ball.

9.14

Alas, Prasena was not seen anymore,
No one had heard of his where about,
With this in mind and deep concern,
Satrajit swiftly went to the woods and returned.

9.15

Thinking that his brother is no more,
He returned to his own residence,
After a bath he held all rituals, needed;
He remained in grief and tears.

9.16

He said this to his relatives:
"Our fate is due to past wrong actions,
We know not the cause of his demise,
Thinking of it one may gain the clue.

9.17

It was the childishness due to age,
That caused him to take this hunt,

Perhaps it was Syamantaka, the gem,
That caused harm to fell that boy.

9.18

A person had come to ask me,
Early - when the gem, he saw,
If one did search that source,
Things will become clear for sure.

9.19

Though one knows the reason why,
The lead is to a place most unspeakable,
It is the fence itself that is encroaching,
On the crop that was sown to protect.

9.20

Our misfortunes are not over yet,
Within my heart I fear the worst,
Those who should protect from harm,
They have come to be the cause of it".

9.21

All the people who dwell in the city,
Hearing such words of Satrajit,
Created a gossip heard amongst them,
And they spread it quickly all around.

9.22

"Have you not heard this special news?
Not easy to live in this land no more,
A Yadava was isolated on a hunt;
He was separated from the group.

9.23

Then, some one came towards him,
And killed him by stabbing him,
The jewel that around his neck he wore,
He stole it and went his way".

9.24

"Who was it that killed Prasena"?
"He that killed Prasena was surely God",
"That I know is the spiritual truth,
My question is: Do you really know"?

9.25

"I will not speak who I know it to be",
"What be the reason for not divulging it"?
"If he who is supreme commits a crime,
Will anyone say that act is wrong?

9.26

"Can you not tell me that little secret"?
"There is no reason why you need not know,

But, by and by, when other people hear,
I will be blamed for spreading the tale".

9.27

"By you I swear; nay, on my two eyes swear,
I will not divulge what you say to any one",
"In that case, hear what I here say,
It was a willful act by Krishna, for sure"!

9.28

"Some time ago Krishna had asked,
Then the Yadava did not comply,
Will those who beg for things on sight,
Fail to steal when proper time arrives"?

9.29

"Those traits seen during early childhood,
Will they be forgotten during later life?
If strychnine seeds are put in milk,
Will bitterness goes away in time"?

9.30

"Sorrow is not the loss of gem,
With effort, lost wealth can be gained,
It is sad that Syamantaka be the cause,
For the death of that young boy"

9.31

"I will say what is in my mind,
That people with wealth need to do,
From this land, with quick effort,
Move their wealth, to some where else".

9.32

 "A place where stealing is done at noon,
Is it safe to store, wealth and jewelry"?
In an extensive way, over all the land,
Such tasteless talks began to spread.

9.33

The cow that walks in front,
Will be followed by other cows,
The gossip that was created by one,
Countless others will spread it around.

9.34

One day, Krishna, the lord of the world,
In an effort to end these reproaches,
Accompanied by four or five Yadavas,
He wandered about in the forest.

9.35

Soon he saw the dead body of Prasena,
And secondly the body of the lion, as well,

Later, following the foot steps there,
He reached the mouth of a depthless cave.

9.36

The mother of the ape-child in play,
On seeing Krishna cried aloud,
And hearing the cries thereafter,
Jambavan came forth quickly.

9.37

"Hark! Who enters my cave?
He will be destroyed by me now,
I am the servant of great Lord Rama,
Once he ruled the seven worlds.

9.38

Hark: Bearing the arrows of Ravana,
My chest was terribly torn in the past,
Note this, that even to this day,
The scars of the wounds are not faded.

9.39

By the blessings of Lord Rama,
I have gained immunity from ailments,
Have you not heard of one,
Named Jambavan; a gallant warrior?

9.40

I am that ape-lord who with bare hands,
Beat to death many burly Rakshasas,
Do not let the feeling grow within,
You are greater than this Jambavan.

9.41

Tarry not, if thy life thou value,
I'll forgive thee for thy actions now,
Or, are thou in error, you imbecile,
Wanting to go to the land of the dead?

9.42

If any one walks in without decorum,
Then this prince of apes will take action,
Walk out from this cave of mine -
Or enter even where death has no access".

9.43

Having said so, the aged ape-lord,
Angry, and with his knuckles curled,
Thumped the chest of Krishna,
Thunderously roaring like a lion.

9.44

Krishna bore five or six of blows,
With the demeanor of a mighty lion,

And with a faint and handsome smile,
He joined the fray, in a casual mode.

9.45

They boxed and with their knees,
They kicked; scratched with their nails;
Bit each other; and with many broken trees,
They fought a mighty battle.

9.46

Then, all the globes shook vehemently,
Quickly, the oceans were in turbulence,
Beasts like the lions became tame,
And the place around was bare of trees.

9.47

The battle raged with no respite,
For fifteen, five and eight more days,
In a faint the old man fell on the turf,
And he raised his eyelids with his hands.

9.48

Then he realized the total truth,
Joyfully he bowed and began to praise,
"For the actions caused by my pride,
Forgive, for ever, my wrongful acts.

9.49

You were the Fish and the Turtle as well,
Then you assumed the form of the Boar,
You were the great and mighty Lion, too,
Oh, Great Soul, you became Vamana in form.

9.50

To this earth you came as Bhargava Rama,
Oh Lord of Lakshmi, you were Raghava Rama, too,
Here now you are also as the blue-robbed Rama,
Oh Primordial Noble One, obeisance to you.

9.51

I now know that you were as Krishna born,
To destroy Kamsa and the likes,
You are alert to protect us from worldly woes,
I bow to you, dark skinned as the clouds".

9.52

Having praised thus, he gave with joy,
His daughter, Jambavati, and the gem,
The aged one then respectfully parted,
And, Krishna, delighted, came away.

9.53

Having gone to the abode of Satrajit,
Krishna, gave to Satrajit, the gem-stone,

Who, with discomfort, shame and fear,
He bowed to Krishna and said as follows:

9.54

"Krishna, great sorrow has come to me,
This evil fate is not of minor make,
Without correctness I spoke too much,
I bow to thee who have much forbearance.

9.55

Forgive me for my wrongful deeds,
Protect me from all harm, Oh Krishna",
So saying he gave his daughter Satyabhama,
And he also gave the gem as well.

9.56

Krishna was most happy in obtaining,
The splendidly beautiful Satyabhama,
And returning the gem to Satrajit,
Krishna quickly returned to his abode.

9.57

Krishna gladly married Satyabhama,
And also the doe-eyed Jambavathi,
Born on earth, like the nectarine moon,
He lived happily in his abode.

9.58

At that time the cruel Kauravas,
Had built, a mansion made of lacquer,
It was learned, that housed in that,
The Pandavas were burned to death.

9.59

Krishna on hearing this news,
Departed quickly; at which time,
Satrajit was killed and the gem taken,
By, some one named Shatadhanva.

9.60

The gossip spread around the land, was:
"It was by Akrura's and Krithavarma's deceit,
That Shatadhvana killed Satrajit",
Satyabhama was grief stricken, thereby.

9.61

While Sri Krishna was living outside,
Satyabhama went to him in grief,
And told Krishna of her father's death,
Thus angered, Krishna killed Satadhanva.

9.62

Due to Syamanthaka, there is bad luck,
To live here is laden with sadness,

Thinking so, Rama decided to leave,
And live in the city of Mithila, instead.

9.63

Rama called for Duryodhana to attend -
During those days of despondency - to amuse,
By teaching his student in mace-combat,
And thus he lived there contentedly.

9.64

To disperse the rumour it was Akrura,
The one who by Krishna's order did the cruel deed,
Krishna brought him from a far off land,
And, Akrura displayed the gem for all to see.

9.65

Thus, that which was the cause of misfortune,
Yet, that which causes all minds to lust,
Krishna asked that that gem be held,
By Akrura, the one with a sterling mind.

9.66

To go to the wedding in the land of Drupada,
Krishna, the embodiment of happiness,
And joy and the one with the smiling face,
He proceeded quickly with Satyabhama.

9.67

For the children of Kunti, he helped to build,
An affluent city named Indraprasta,
That beautiful city was like the place of Indra,
Afterwards, Krishna went back to Dwaraka.

9.68

After living in happiness for some years,
At the expansive palace thereby,
Arjuna, infatuated with the maiden,
Dressed as a saint, he came to Dwaraka.

9.69

Subhadra, who was his own sister,
Krishna gave to Arjuna in marriage,
This he did when the city deserted,
And all the people had gone to a carnival.

9.70

Arjuna, Subhadra's beloved -
Son of Indra - stayed at Indraprasta,
And one day as he was living happily there,
The Lord, who is the embodiment of joy,
On short notice, along with his contingent,
And Balarama, of great prowess,
With Krishna – World's Happiness,
All of them, with joy, came to Arjuna's place.

9.71

On the shores of Kalindi,
He saw Kalindi, playing,
And Krishna, who has the color,
Of dark blue clouds - married her,
After the sugar-cane forest, was,
Quickly reduced to ashes by a great fire,
Krishna, with the playfully delightful,
Kalindi at his side went to his abode.

9.72

From the land of Avanti, the damsel Mithravinda,
Was quickly taken by Krishna, with him,
Later, he tied seven bullocks securely,
And won Satya to wed, and lived happily.

9.73

Bhadra, whose brother was Santardha,
She with a graceful form like kalpaka vine,
A princess of delightful character,
Krishna, of excellent mind, wed and lived happily.

9.74

The fish that were reflected in the waters,
As targets, he cut with his arrows,
He married the daughter of the king of Madra,
Lakshana, with desirable features,
Thusly, having obtained eight wives,

To form an impeccable group,
And he enjoyed this charming team,
That worthy wearer of forest flower garland.

battles with narakasura and banasura

10.1

An Asura named, Naraka, son of Earth,
He who set fear in people's minds,
Captured a group of beautiful maidens,
And he took them to his palace to keep.

10.2

Overcoming the power of Indra,
He attacked the land of the gods,
From one of Indra's emissaries,
Krishna heard all the news.

10.3

Krishna, along with Satyabhama,
Riding on the swift king of birds,
And when entering the city of his enemy,
He showered arrows at Naraka in haste.

10.4

Realizing that the fortresses of fire, water,
Mountain were all crossed by Krishna,
The five-headed, Murasura, came quickly,
And he came with great anger.

10.5

Taking up the powerful discus of Vishnu,
He cut off the heads of Mura, in battle,
And the five heads, severed from the body,
Fell trembling, on the ground, like mountains.

10.6

The angry chieftain, Narakasura,
Quickly reached the battle field,
And showering so many arrows,
He attacked all ten directions.

10.7

The king of birds with much ferocity,
Started to flap his mighty wings,
Then with thousands of arrows at once,
That low Asura began to throw.

10.8

Then, Garuda retreated briefly,
And at that time Krishna felt faint,

So, Satyabhama, picking up the bow,
She faced Naraka, the enemy of the gods.

10.9

Struck by the arrows of Satyabhama,
The body of Narakasura was cut deeply,
Will the proud and great Asura,
Accept defeat from a beautiful dame?

10.10

"Stop, you fickle maid, what right,
Do you have, to hold a bow in battle?
If you do not heed my advice,
I will not pause to end your life".

10.11

Saying these word in arrogance,
Naraka, began to engage in battle,
Then, the enemy of Asuras, Krishna,
Picked up his discus and gave battle.

10.12

Quickly, Krishna, using the discus,
Severed Naraka's head from his body,
Thereafter, all the soldiers in arms,
Fell dead there on the battle field.

10.13

Krishna, abiding the Earth Goddess' wish,
Reduced the weight of evil thus,
Then, Bhagadatha, son of Naraka,
Krishna anointed as king of the realm.

10.14

Gleefully, Krishna made as his,
All, excepting a single elephant,
Behold, there are many maidens,
Captured by Naraka and held.

10.15

Krishna, took to his residence,
The sixteen thousand maidens,
Then, happily, Krishna returned two earrings,
Once taken from Aditi as he visited heaven.

10.16

He returned the two earrings,
That was taken by force by Naraka,
In total happiness for two months,
The dark skinned Krishna lived in heaven.

10.17

The dark-haired beauty, Satyabhama,
Fell fondly in want, when she saw,

The tree-of-plenty, Indra's Parijatham,
And Krishna took it as they returned.

10.18

The army of Devas so assembled,
Krishna defeated them in battle,
And in front of Satyabhama's yard,
The tree-of-plenty was planted.

10.19

In that place, as the wedding jubilations,
For the ten-thousand maidens,
Were being held - the handsome,
Krishna was seen to shine in all his glory.

10.20

The sage Narada, as an inquirer,
Came by, unknown to anyone,
And with a sense of curiosity,
He visited different homes of Krishna,

10.21

At every home the sage Narada saw,
Krishna with a smiling face,
Seeing this, on and on, the sage was aghast,
And he praised, respectfully, and left.

10.22

Kama, burned by fire from the third eye,
He who caps the sickle-moon,
In one of Rukmini's birthing,
Kama was born as her son.

10.23

Sambara Asura, using his magic,
Stole the baby from the mother's lap,
And threw the son of Krishna,
Into the ocean and then ran away.

10.24

A fish swallowed the child,
And it wandered around in the sea,
Then one of the fisher-men,
Netted the fish, soon there after.

10.25

The fisherman, picked it from the net,
And he and a local chieftain,
Offered the fish to an Asura,
Sambara, by name, who lived by the sea.

10.26

Following Narada's promptings,
Was residing in the home of Sambara,

The beautiful Ratidevi, with hope,
So that she can be with Kama, the Cupid.

10.27

Ratidevi, was by the base Asura given,
The task of working in the kitchen,
"Cook this to the best you can",
Ordered Sambara, and gave her the fish.

10.28

Without trouble, when she cut open,
The bloated stomach of the fish,
A beautiful little baby boy,
The woman found inside.

10.29

She picked the child by her hands,
And began to take care of the child,
Then, the sage Narada came quickly,
He told the cultured lady the following:

10.30

"Oh, wife of Kama, who holds five arrows,
This is Kama, the one with a beautiful face,
So, pretty lady, this is your husband,
Rear him up, without any concern.

10.31

Have you forgotten those words?
That I told you earlier?
Cupid, your beloved husband,
He has come to be with you now.

10.32

This boy is the offspring of,
Rukmini and Krishna, of full virtue,
Oh, damsels of good words, follow my advice,
Only good comes to you for doing so.

10.33

The evil desires of Sambara Asura,
Will soon be terminated by Kama",
Having said these words,
He vanished from the scene.

10.34

Day by day, she was getting more attached,
This was well understood by the boy,
In question why this was going on,
He asked Rati the following words:

10.35

"Oh, mother, am I not your son,
How can I but remember that?

Need you feel such amorous love to me?
I see that from your glances towards me.

10.36

Exceeding normal fondness towards a son,
What is the cause for this excessive love?"
In response to what was said hereby,
Rati gave response to that, thusly:

10.37

"The sage Narada has reiterated,
That you are my lawful husband,
Due to the strength of your past life,
You are reborn as Kama once again.

10.38

Listen to me, Oh, son of Krishna,
Sambara Asura, is your true enemy,
After destroying Sambara Asura,
We shall go to Krishna's place".

10.39

Hearing the words of the lovely lady,
The boy called out loudly with pride,
"Come to battle, Oh, Sambara,
Your evil works will soon be at an end.

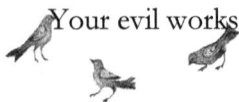

10.40

I am the son of Krishna,
You threw into the ocean, for sure,
Your arrogance will end in the battle,
Come to fight me, Oh, Sambara".

10.41

When Sambara Asura heard, these words,
From the angry son of Krishna,
He shouted so loudly,
As to break the eight regions, and said:

10.42

"Tarry a little, you ill tempered boy,
I have no compunction in killing you,
Pick up and string your bow,
And be prepared to go to hell.

10.43

Your sugar-cane bow has no strength,
Why then are you boasting, you imbecile?
Observe then that by cutting your head,
My fame will increase, be sure of that.

10.44

Will a lion that relishes,
Splitting the forehead of an elephant,

Have concern in front of a fawn?
Will a rabbit be able to kill a tusker"?

10.45

Anger and in strength came Sambara,
Having lost his senses due to pride,
He began the combat with Krishna's son,
Using weapons which his teacher blessed.

10.46

Krishna's son used his own illusions,
To thwart the illusions by the Asura,
And with cutting arrows with arrows,
He continued to battle without qualm.

10.47

Chariot, thousands of weapons, horses,
Solid Breast-plate, arrow-plate and bow,
A host of army, all these and more,
Kama, the Cupid, destroyed in battle.

10.48

The demon that was like a lion,
He destroyed, in battle; and the army too,
Looking like the chief of the army of the gods,
Kama reached Dwaraka City.

10.49

When Pradyumna, was coming with Rati,
People of the city were confused,
Was Krishna returning with a new maiden?
So the citizenry wondered at that site.

10.50

Who is this – handsome; dark as the clouds;
Victor of the world and wide-eyed one –
In appearance like handsome Krishna;
So, Rukmini was for long, perplexed.

10.51

At this time, Narada arrived and said:
"Daughter of Vidarbha, you of perfect body,
He who is of the colour of dark clouds,
Surely is your son, the beautiful Kama.

10.52

You of the flirting eyes! Earlier, during birth,
The wicked, Sambara, had thrown him in the sea,
But, now after quickly killing the demon,
That handsome man has returned to your midst.

10.53

Ratidevi is the one who is his true wife,
She is chaste and unapproachable to any.

Now, live your life happily,
O lady of sweet eyes, with him and the lady here".

10.54

Having said that, that great sage left,
Thence forth, Lord Krishna and Rukmini,
Along with Pradyumna and Ratidevi,
They all lived happily in the royal house.

10.55

Anirudha, son of Pradyumna, was born soon,
With the body glow like the moon in full,
Pradyumna, kidnapped the daughter of Rukmi,
And he carried her away from Vidarbha palace.

10.56

At the same time, Anirudha, carried off,
The grand-daughter of Rukmi,
Seeing these proper marriage wows,
The clans of Yadu and Vrishni, joined happily.

10.57

At that festive time, while playing dice,
Balarama and none other, with great anger,
And without hesitation slew Rukmi,
Those in anger treat even trivial, seriously.

10.58

Usha, with a face glowing like the moon,
The daughter of Banasura,
By god's grace, saw Anirudha, with dark hair,
In a dream; and she woke up feeling lonely.

10.59

"Oh, beautiful like Cupid in form,
Handsomest in the world, where are you now"?
Her companion, Citralekha, hearing her cries,
Asked quickly, "Who is this nobleman"?

10.60

"I saw today, Oh, beautiful, Citralekha,
In looks he is handsome, like a new Cupid,
It was fortunate that I saw him in my dream,
But, it is less so, since I've lost him since".

10.61

Thereafter, Citralekha, drew paintings,
Of all the handsome men in the realm,
By and by, while looking at the paintings,
The young woman saw Anirudha among them.

10.62

Seeing the love-pangs of Usha on viewing,
The portrait of Anirudha, Citralekha said:

"Oh, Usha, do not feel sadness in your heart,
For, I shall bring here the son of Cupid".

10.63

Following on her words, Citralekha,
Quickly, reached Krishna's mansion at night,
And using yogic powers, that companion,
He gently, brought Anirudha there, secretly.

10.64

With the son of the son of Krishna,
Brought by Kumbhanda's daughter's magic,
A secret amorous interlude was held,
By the lotus eyed daughter of Bana.

10.65

When Bana was, by a servant, informed,
Of a stranger in the lady's rooms,
He saw the son of the son of Krishna,
Playing dice in there.

10.66

Furious, Bana, engaged in battle;
Anirudha, opposed him, haughtily,
In fight, he tied the boy, with snake-arrows,
And he hid him at a place, from common view.

10.67

Hearing from Narada, of his son's captivity,
Krishna and Balarama with great anger,
And with the always-ready Yadava army,
They surrounded the city of Shonitapura.

10.68

The guardian of the city of Banasura,
The three-eyed Shiva, also joined the fight,
Pradyumna and Guha fought each other;
Quickly Krishna opposed Siva.

10.69

Kumbhanda and Balarama began to fight,
Kumbodhara and others joined Asura's army,
And how loud indeed were the war cries -
Made by, Bhrungeeriti, Bhrumgi, Vasuki and Ganesha?

10.70

Then, the whole army of Siva,
Quickly withdrew from battle and stood afar,
At that time, the son of Bali,
Bana came face to face to fight Krishna.

10.71

Five hundred bows were cut asunder,
By Krishna on the battle field,

Kottavi, came forth to halt the fight,
Then, Bana ran from the battle-field.

10.72

The deadly fever-of-Siva, when sent,
The army of Krishna began to weaken,
But, the fever-of-Vishnu, overcame it,
At end, Siva's army fell at Vishnu's feet.

10.73

Krishna addressed the Fever-of-Siva,
"Enough of your weakening efforts,
For those who meditate on me,
They will not suffer the discomfort of illness".

10.74

Later on, when Banasura, began,
To engage in heavy fighting with Krishna,
Krishna quickly took,
To cutting those terrible arms of Bana.

10.75

Ceding to the wishes of Lord Siva,
Krishna, did not cut the last four arms of Bana,
Then Banasura, with great devotion,
Spoke praise to Krishna, as Lord Vishnu.

10.76

"Obeisance to you, Krishna, Sea of Mercy,
Obeisance to you, Govinda; Lord Vishnu,
You who shine in the hearts of men,
Forgive me for my transgressions.

10.77

Hark; you of the color of new rain clouds,
I give my daughter, to your son's son,
He may in marriage accept my daughter,
Saying thus he gave up his child.

10.78

Happily, Krishna, along with,
His son and the joyful husband of Usha;
Many units and those of the clan of Vrishni,
Under the leadership of Balarama;
All together, went to his lovely residence,
Rounded by the sea;
And with those close to him,
He lived for many days with sportive joy.

other adventures and the great battle

11.1

At that time, wanting to play in the woods,
The children of Krishna, in formation,
Came, to a steep mountain side,
Where there was an entrance to a well.

11.2

A small lizard had fallen in the well,
And in vain it was trying to climb ashore,
And in vain the children tried to help,
Hearing the children; Krishna arrived.

11.3

Krishna, brought it ashore and in sight of all,
Even as the children gazed,
It changed its lizard form,
And it glowed to the body of a king.

11.4

With humility, the king addressed:
"Oh Sea of Kindness, Lord of the World,
To thee I bow; a king named Nruga am I,
Listen to the sins of my life before.

11.5

I draped two horns and four hoofs too,
In gold that shimmered with brightness,
And gave in fashion many such cows,
To Brahmins who were very chaste.

11.6

Once, to a learned Brahmin, I gave,
A cow, which retuned to the herd,
Then, hastily, not understanding such,
I gave the same to another priestly man.

11.7

Thereafter, that Brahmin, owner of the cow,
Came to me and said these angry words,
"What is this: You take, what you give, away?
Was what you did any good, you sinful one?

11.8

Oh King, you are indeed a hefty miser -
You have no hardship to conduct charity,

By giving the same cow to many people,
Hope you to gain salvation to heaven"?

11.9

More than once I said, humbly, to him,
I will give him wealth and also many cows,
"Know this Oh Brahmin, I am held,
By what has occurred - I seek forgiveness".

11.10

"Do not speak about all these to me,
Just give what was justly given to me",
Thus, angrily, that Brahmin said to me,
Thereupon, I spoke to the other Priest:

11.11

"I will give you a hundred thousand cows,
In exchange give me back the one I gave",
"You need not give me one in exchange,
This one is mine": So said that obstinate one.

11.12

Then, I reached a state of depression;
For that Brahmin with poisonous anger grown,
Cursed me thus: "For having given my cow,
To another, you will as a lizard live.

11.13

You shall fall into that deep rotten well",
"So said that Brahmin to me then,
And, I went forth in the form of a lizard,
I fell into this well; such then is my tale.

11.14

Now, by your touch Oh, Lord Krishna,
My sins have all been washed away,
Obeisance, to you Oh, merciful Lord;
More and more, to you, I bow".

11.15

Krishna said to the king who praised him,
"You may live in tranquility, Oh King,
Go forth to your own residence,
You will gain immense wealth and comfort".

11.16

The king left after repeated bows,
And Krishna also left for his residence,
He called together the three clans of Yadu,
The lord of the worlds said thus to them:

11.17

"Heard you not the root of the king's curse?
Brahmins are the only gods of earth,

None should covet a Brahmin's ownership,
None should hinder a Brahmin's way of life".

11.18

Those devoted to Brahmins on this earth,
Are men of character and loved by me,
Those of you who yearn my blessing,
Meet the need, if Brahmins wants are met".

11.19

What one gives to them pleases me most,
They are the embodiment of the Trinity,
He who does those nasty things to them,
Into the pits of hell, they quickly fall.

11.20

When learned Brahmins come your way,
People should with respect take,
Inviting, worshipping and being humble,
It is equal to the worship of the Trinity".

11.21

Krishna having said such truthful words,
Showed them the path to greater devotion,
Thereafter, Balarama, with happiness,
To the land of the Gopas he went, accordingly.

11.22

Balarama frolicked at the homes of the Gopis,
And traveled to the woods next to Kalindi,
When Kalindi failed to respond to his call,
He quickly cut her arrogance and lived contented.

11.23

In due course, the messenger sent by,
Paundraka Vaasudeva, arrived at Dwaraka,
He stood humbly facing Krishna,
And he said these words, clearly.

11.24

"The ferocious Paundraka Vaasudeva,
Has sent me to convey these words:
'Understand this Krishna, there exists,
Only one Vaasudeva – that great one, I am.

11.25

I hold in my hands, conch and the discus,
I have in hand, the mace and the lotus,
On my chest, Kaustubha and the garland;
Many other magnificent items too.

11.26

Boast not, you are the lord of the world,
And thereby walk in arrogance',

All these to inform you, here, quickly;
Thus advises Paundraka to you".

11.27

Krishna sent the messenger with no reply,
But, Krishna, was with anger mounting,
With the great Yadava army,
He marched to the land of Paundraka.

11.28

Behold, the foolish Paundraka Vasudeva,
Living in the form of Lord Vishnu,
In that style was he dressed,
He even had, to form, a bed-of-snake.

11.29

With two extra wooden hands,
And a shining jewel for Kausthbha,
One as Lakshmi, and the other Earth,
He had them, one on either side.

11.30

A white conch and an iron discus,
Shining ear-drops though imitations,
All this Krishna saw with rising anger,
And he prepared to kill him right away.

11.31

Holding an iron discus in a wooden arm,
The base Paundraka came running forward,
Krishna using his discus, Sudarshana,
Killed him; his army too was destroyed.

11.32

Krishna's arrow traveled quickly,
To where the King of Kasi lived - to kill,
Happily, he proceeded to Dwaraka,
Blissfully, he arrived there, in time.

11.33

That time, the son of the King of Kasi,
Sudaksina, sorrowed by his father's death,
Went to do penance to Lord Shiva,
And he gained the services of Krutriya.

11.34

Krutriya reached the city of Krishna,
With her gang of demons and ghosts,
At the time when Krishna was playing dice,
Without concern he threw his discus swiftly.

11.35

Sudarshana went and chased and burned,
Kruthriya, and the demon group,

Then it burned Sudaksina and Kasi city;
Victorious, it came back to Krishna.

11.36

After much time, Rama with the Gopis,
Returned to Dwaraka to enjoy further,
Came to the city, a friend of Narakasura,
A quarrelsome monkey named Vivida.

11.37

He stood in the waters of the sea,
And scooped waters to four directions,
Then, buildings and healthy trees as well,
Were uprooted and made to fall to ground.

11.38

People who lived in the houses,
Were killed, bitten and eaten by the ape,
He burned the homes of noble Brahmins,
That wicked one moved to the main city.

11.39

Realizing that Balarama was,
In company of beautiful maidens,
And satiated with drinking wine,
Vivida, that strong ape, came, stealthily by.

11.40

When the maidens looked as he cried aloud,
He showed his teeth and climbed a tree,
Coming close he drank wine from the jar,
Intoxicated he began to play about.

11.41

Seeing the prowess of the monkey,
The pretty women, in anxiety, lived,
Seeing this and being angry on account,
Balarama took out his weapon - mace.

11.42

"Come hither, you monkey-beast,
Your end is near due to your fickle acts,
Dare, block this": So saying, and quickly,
He struck the monkey's head with a blow.

11.43

The fight began with Rama and the ape,
And the world shook and the sea did froth,
They struck, chased, boxed, toppled,
Dragged and fought each other, thus.

11.44

The white body of Balarama,
When it was splashed by the ape's blood,

Looked, in battle, like an autumn cloud,
That was tinged with the rays of the rising sun.

11.45

With the heavy mace, the evil one,
Was hit on the head and the monkey killed,
The anger born of battle was soon subdued,
And he lived in tranquil peace, thereafter.

11.46

Thereafter, the son of Jambavati,
The able Samban, went for the betrothal,
Of the Kuru king's daughter; tried to steal her,
And was caught and tied by Duryodhana.

11.47

Hearing this news, Rama went there,
Gave proper advice; was rejected by Kuru,
Then, with increased anger showing,
He shook the Kuru City with his plough.

11.48

Slowly, he began to uproot the city,
And throw it into the River Ganga,
The fearful clan of Duryodhana,
Fell at his feet and sought mercy.

11.49

Following this, Duryodhana gave,
His daughter Lakshana to Samban,
Pleased with this, Balarama,
Along with Samban, went to his home.

11.50

Once, during the solar eclipse,
Krishna went along, with his wives,
To bathe in the glorious five rivers,
And he gave away much gold in charity.

11.51

At that time, the five sons of Pandu,
And along with them Pancali too,
In their minds was much curious news,
They spent time talking of many such.

11.52

Once at that time, Pancali told,
Krishna's wives, the sublime truth,
Of who Krishna was; soon after,
Krishna left, to his own abode.

11.53

Krishna went to Ambadi, where,
The happy maidens had once doted on him,

He spent three months in their company,
And he left for Dwaraka, soon there after.

11.54

In the end, those kings whom,
King Jarasandha, had held captives,
Sent their trusted messenger one day,
And the immortal Narada also arrived.

11.55

The messenger told of the kings' suffering,
The sage told of the Pandavas' desire,
Krishna understood both concerns,
And he agreed to bring them both to end.

11.56

"It is suitable for us that Jarasandha die,
It is proper, Yudhistira hold his royal sacrifice,
Both are equal in importance to us,
If one is done the other will happen too".

11.57

If Yudhistira's yaga comes to be,
Then killing Jarasandha can also happen,
Having quickly decided so in mind,
Krishna went to the home of Yudhistira.

11.58

He reached the city of Indraprasta,
Krishna, along with all his wives,
After that, he and Bhimasena,
And Arjuna – were three of equal mind.

11.59

The three went to the city of Magadha,
Dressed as Brahmins and began to fight,
Quickly, with Jarasandha and Bhima,
A horrid battle with the mace began.

11.60

Following Krishna's advice of guile;
Gaining the stratagem to kill the enemy,
In battle, Jarasandha's body, was by Bhima,
Torn apart and quickly destroyed.

11.61

The captive kings held in the dungeon,
Were unchained and set free, all at once,
He gave the country to his son, Sahadeva,
Victorious, Krishna came away, contented.

11.62

When the foremost of emperors, performed,
The royal sacrifice, based on his prowess,

Then, among many nobles, Krishna was,
By Yudhistira, the virtuous, revered most.

11.63

"With so many noble kings looking on,
Why grant the cow-herder such respect?"
With such abusive words, Sishupala came,
Then, angry Arjuna readied to fight.

11.64

Quickly did Krishna, red-eyed with anger,
Sever the head of the Chedi King,
Then, Jaya, who had passed three births,
With Krishna's self, he gracefully merged.

11.65

King of kings, Yudhistira,
Did the royal rituals with awe,
He went and stayed at the royal hall,
That the Maya Asura had built.

11.66

Krishna, the Lord of the Worlds,
Bhima, Arjuna, Nakula and others,
Pancali and many, many,
Wise men were in the assembly.

11.67

In places there was water or just land,
Such magic illusion puzzled Duryodhana,
He came with pride and jealousy,
Fell in the water and angrily went away.

11.68

King Salva, having prayed to Siva,
Received the flying chariot - by his grace,
And went to Krishna's city,
With an extensive army of soldiers,
Pradyumna, in the middle of the battle,
Killed the king's minister,
And held battle with Salva,
For twenty seven days.

11.69

During this time, Krishna, like a lion,
That kills its enemy - the elephant;
Took the form of Gopala for mirth,
Along with Balarama, joined the battle,
Krishna cut the fearful flying machine,
With his discus and threw it in the sea,
Later, he destroyed the army,
And he killed King Salva too.

11.70

Then, while waiting, there appeared,

The violently angry, Danthavaktra,
Who, mighty like the lion,
And Krishna killed him with the mace,
And, quickly, at the end of three births,
Vijaya was sent to his own dwelling place,
Krishna, god of gods, who protects sages,
He lived happily in his city.

11.71

Krishna, gave binding support when Pancali,
In trouble, was dragged by hair and garb;
Krishna, gave further needed council,
After the thirteen year sojourn,
He acted as the mediator, at the Kuru Hall,
To convey the proper requests;
Was angered with the rejection of Duryodhana,
So he assumed the all destroying cosmic form.

11.72

In the terrible Bharata battle,
On victorious Arjuna's chariot,
The wielder of the discus, took upon,
The esteemed position, of a charioteer;
Having given Bhishma, Drona, Kripa,
And others, unreserved salvation,
The heavy burden on the Earth,
Due to evil men, he reduced.

11.73

At the time when the battle started,
Balarama, went on a pilgrimage,
To the forest named Vymisham,
And paid respect to the sages in the woods,
And upon seeing his charioteer,
Not standing up, he killed him quickly,
Then feeling remorse,
He made that man's son, his charioteer.

11.74

Most wicked-minded and cruel, Valkalasura,
Was disrupting the yagas; and Balarama,
Killed, him on a full-moon day,
And reinstated the sacrificial rites as before,
Then, he went to Kaveri, Sarasvati, Yamuna,
Ganga and also to Godavari,
After having gained salvation by pilgrimage,
He returned to native Kurukshetra.

11.75

At that time, seeing the combat between,
Bhima and Duryodhana, and convinced,
That neither will heed his words,
Rama returned to Dwaraka;
When the battle ended, Krishna,
Beloved of his devotees, entered the womb,
Of Uttara, to curtail the fire from the arrow,
That came from Drona's son - fiercest of men.

11.76

Absolute salvation was reached, by Bhishma,
The great nobleman; and the duty bound,
Yudhistira established all ruling principles,
To his wish; later, Krishna helped Yudhistira,
To perform three, horse sacrifices;
And after all this was properly done,
Krishna, the supreme lord,
Left in happiness, to live in Dwaraka.

two final stories

12.1

Due to his good conduct, he was well known,
He was a Brahmin by name Kucela,
Though very poor, he lived with self control,
Close to Sandeepani's place of stay.

12.2

Distraught at seeing the children,
So weakened by hunger,
The Brahmin's wife, with no hesitation,
To the well mannered Brahmin, said:

12.3

"Though we are poor, and own so little,
There are not many, who have any less,
Understand my lord, for us now,
We have no means for a daily meal.

12.4

When in search of food I go,
The neighbours tell me there is no food,
If not, they give a small measure of rice,
Be it grain, with husk, so late at night.

12.5

A small measure of rice must last a day,
For five or six to consume,
When the sun rise in the east, my children,
Hold my feet and cry, my husband!

12.6

Other people sell their wares,
To provide for the welfare of their own,
It would seem that you, Oh Brahmin,
Have no desire to care for yours.

12.7

Those who seek refuge in the divine,
Will gain from him with no conditions,
It is said, that the tender-hearted Krishna,
Was once a close friend of yours?

12.8

He has wed to two times eight thousand,
And eight more – according to proper norms,

All the wealth and welfare that they want,
He gives them without halt.

12.9

Go thou and come after seeing him,
Perhaps he may give to meet our needs,
The husband of the Goddess of Wealth,
He'll show compassion to our lowly state.

12.10

Without pause the Brahmin said:
"He who is Infinite, may grant us wealth,
But knowing that wealth just breeds evil,
I refrain from yearning for it, my wife!

12.11

The rich man will have many enemies,
His mind will be filled with much fear,
He will never be satiated by wants,
Increased wealth will also raise deceit.

12.12

To those who barely make a living,
To those who partake of daily meals,
To those who amassed much wealth,
To all sorrow come without a break.

12.13

Be as it may, I shall go and come,
If he gives, then, I shall bring it here,
If not, I will merely go to see,
Krishna's smiling pleasant face.

12.14

Even as the Brahmin was speaking,
At the corner of a dirty rag,
A scoop of beaten rice was tied,
Bowing to his feet she gave and let him leave.

12.15

The Brahmin, Kucela, went happily,
And entered Krishna's residence,
When Krishna saw him coming,
He held his hands; sat next to him.

12.16

Krishna after receiving him with due honor,
Performed the eight fold rites for a Brahmin, true,
And his chief consort, Rukmini fanned the guest,
For which the Brahmin thanked the Gods.

12.17

Krishna spoke to Kucela,
Joyfully, on various matters:

"Oh, Brahmin, have you forgotten,
The past: we lived in our teacher's place?

12.18

When we went to the woods to gather,
Drift-wood – a sudden rain dowsed us,
We lost our way, and as we wandered,
For time to come, wet and weary.

12.19

The sage returned to look for us,
And when he saw us on the road,
He blessed us in appropriate style,
Kucela, do you remember this"?

12.20

Krishna, loosened the rag and ate,
A handful of the beaten rice,
When he reached for a second hold,
Rukmini held his hand.

12.21

After having had his food, with Krishna,
With happiness in his mind he stayed,
The next day he woke and wished good bye,
Kucela was so gratified, and left for home.

12.22

"Had I sought some wealth from Krishna,
He would never have said no for sure,
Being happily involved with my talks,
I did forgot, my own poor welfare.

12.23

Why, Krishna did not even ask,
About the well fare of my home,
Had I spoken without asked,
What indeed would the lord have thought?

12.24

What indeed can I reply,
To my dear wife when asked about:
'I sadly did not quite remember,
My household waits for my return'".

12.25

As he was walking, thinking thus,
He beheld a magnificent gate,
And he also saw tall buildings,
That glowed with jewels and pearls, as well.

12.26

Gardens and warehouses,
Shining gold homes, too, he saw,

Gem studded halls to play and dance,
And shiny bathing pools, he saw.

12.27

Did I reach here having lost my way?
To whom belongs this heavenly house?
Not only that, but from a distance, comes,
A lovely maiden ornately dressed.

12.28

"Oh, Krishna, is that truly my wife,
Who comes from inside the yonder house?
Is this divine magic or my wishful fancy?
I bow to you, Govinda; Muckunda; Vishnu!

12.29

I gather what I've seen till now,
Is but the playful will of Krishna,
The wealth which was given without seeking,
How glorious to see; how wonderful, indeed"?

12.30

Thus satisfied he entered the city.
And with his wife he rejoiced greatly,
Knowing in reality that life was full,
Kucela lived each day; contented.

12.31

Krishna, following Devaki's desire, traveled,
To the lower regions to find the six boys,
Whom Kamsa killed; after Devaki met them,
Krishna took them to Vaikunda.

12.32

Bahulasha was a might king,
Shutadeva was a learned Brahmin,
To grant salvation to these two,
Krishna went to Mithila.

12.33

Krishna split into two identical forms,
He went to two places to accept offerings,
At one place it was milk, honey and ghee,
At the other, it was tubers, water and leaves.

12.34

Equally pleased, he gave them both,
Extended happiness as his blessings,
Krishna, the chaste gem of thought,
To his devotees - went happily to Dwaraka.

12.35

At that time, deeply saddened,
By the loss, of all eight sons,

A Brahmin, crying deeply,
Came to Krishna and told him thus:

12.36

"It is impossible for me, noble Brahmin,
To remove the effects of the fruits of fate",
Then, when Krishna said so,
The Brahmin left, disappointed.

12.37

At that time, Arjuna came to Dwaraka,
That sorrow-filled Brahmin also came,
"Krishna, my ninth child has also died,
I find no place to hide my sorrow?"

12.38

Think of this: It's not one or two,
But, I have lost nine sons,
Are you not moved by this sad news?
Krishna, feel you not this in your mind?

12.39

I am not blessed with the grace of god,
To have a child and to enjoy it well,
To other people who live in your city,
You seem to show no love to any.

12.40

'To me, I am more important':
Truthfully - this is your belief,
Misfortune that comes to many,
Due to lack of feeling, affects you not.

12.41

There are many beautiful women here,
Indeed, you have enormous wealth,
Any worry, even that to speak,
You do not possess, for certain, Krishna".

12.42

Hearing these words of marked displeasure,
Arjuna was angered and spoke to him:
"Oh, Brahmin, enough of your ugly words,
Quickly, I will remove your woes.

12.43

In the battle field, those Kaurava warriors,
Were swiftly done and killed by me,
My fame is vast and ever spreading,
Oh, Brahmin, I am Arjuna, the victorious.

12.44

From now on, from this very day,
Soul of any son of yours is by me guarded,

If not be so, then this my body,
I will, in fire, burn to ashes".

12.45

The Brahmin, having heard this promise,
Went home, with so much happiness,
And Arjuna installed the arrow-cage,
And he stayed guard, outside the house.

12.46

Brahmin's wife at the birthing house,
Gave birth to a wholesome son,
Then, not even the son's body,
They could find for all to view.

12.47

The Brahmin came to complain,
In a dark and somber mood, he said:
"Strange indeed your life story, Arjuna,
You are one without feelings, you imbecile!

12.48

Narrating each of those foolish tales,
You made my heart to flutter,
By your prowess, I did not gain,
My new born son's body, even!

12.49

The boastful words you said took effect,
Go thou and fall into a burning pyre,
Hearing these words, Arjuna,
Returned quickly; not losing pride.

12.50

He searched in nether world and heaven, too,
He searched in the God of Death's abode,
Not succeeding he returned empty,
And he was prepared to self-immolate.

12.51

As he made the preparations,
To leap into the raging fire,
Krishna with a smile on his face,
Quickly, he held Arjuna's hand.

12.52

Then, Krishna had Arjuna climb,
In the chariot, and in a casual way,
He too climbed in a pleasant mood,
They traveled in a northerly route.

12.53

Slowly, they travelled crossed past the worlds,
So did, Krishna and Arjuna,

Further yet, they reached the place,
Without sun's rays; with darkness engulfed.

12.54

By the brightness of the discus, Sudarshana,
The great blackness was removed,
As if by the sun's rays – and then they saw,
Far, far away, the sublime land of Vaikunda.

12.55

Near the shore, where the waves pound,
In the milky ocean, surrounded by luster,
Playful places, gardens, golden trees,
Golden houses of merriment; they saw.

12.56

By flagpoles studded with gems,
With silk banners fluttering freely,
Large structures with tall walls,
Standing loftily; they saw.

12.57

Splendorous with the glow of many gems,
Were the many hoods of the serpent Ananta,
And those noble people who had arrived,
Soon after gaining salvation; they saw.

12.58

They with the discus, conch, lotus, mace,
They with bodies like the dark clouds,
They with four arms, handsome men,
They with the brilliant Kaustubha; they saw.

12.59

With crown, pearls, bracelet, flower garland,
Splendid in wind blown yellow silk robe,
Row upon rows of Vishnu's associates,
In gem studded buildings; they saw.

12.60

Gradually, on the raised serpent coiled bed,
With Goddesses Earth and Lakshmi, at side,
He with the form of immeasurable joy,
The Eternal Universal Being; they saw.

12.61

Getting closer, they could hear the pious,
Saints like Thumburu and Narada, sing,
And, later, in a humble manner,
They stood, by the eternal being.

12.62

Then, on Lord Vishnu's serpent bed,
Gleefully, playing hide and seek,

And with equal joy near Goddess Lakshmi,
Those boys were seen to play.

12.63

Humbly they went, Krishna and Arjuna,
They stood in reverence, with much devotion,
The lord, who for ever sits on the serpent,
Said these words in joy:

12.64

"Oh, Krishna, oh, Arjuna, though you are,
Part of me, yet you are my incarnations,
I say that I have much desired,
Just to see your noble forms.

12.65

Because I wanted to see you quickly,
I, secretly, took away the Brahmin's boys,
Seeing my prowess here, and departing,
You too will gain salvation, soon.

12.66

To reduce the torments of the world,
So much of killing of life forms were done,
And all the sins caused thereby,
Know that on seeing me, they will be purged.

12.67

So, take the children and depart,
And gain the blessings from the Brahmin",
So Lord Vishnu said, and with joy,
He handed them the Brahmin's boys.

12.68

"Son, who your mother and father be"?
So asked Krishna in a merry mood,
Lord Vishnu and Goddess Lakshmi,
That boy pointed to and touched.

12.69

Extending his arm, to pick him gently,
Krishna prepared to do,
Crying, loudly, one of the boys,
Climbed the serpent's hood and lay there.

12.70

With smiles and baby-talks,
Krishna, called a boy to play,
From open daylight the boy ran out,
He hid some where - that one boy.

12.71

Krishna who was overcome with love,
Reached forth to pick the boys,

One of them crawled away on his knees,
The other crept away without regard.

12.72

When Lord Vishnu noticed, that the boys,
Showed no desire to leave the place,
By bringing a measure of illusion to act,
He raised a want in them to return home.

12.73

At that time, the first born boy,
Who walked quickly, went in front,
And his brother and another, went behind,
His brother, brother and his brother too,
Went slowly; the next one waddled by,
And the next went holding for support,
One crawled on his knees,
The last, swam on the ground, fast.

12.74

They swarmed and whirled around,
The esteemed feet of Sri Krishna,
Respectively, the boys thought,
Of their mother and home with desire,
These Brahmin boys, who were so moved,
Were quickly lifted on to the chariot,
Krishna and Arjuna bowed to Vishnu,

And, alas, bade farewell from there.

12.75

Having reached the City of Dwaraka,
They went to the house of the Brahmin,
He who grants happiness always,
Gave, to the Brahmin and his wife,
Their ten sons; and Krishna and Arjuna,
Having gained those many blessings,
From the Brahmin, they excelled brightly.

12.76

"Valour, longevity, fame, strength, wealth,
All these and more you two will gain",
So saying the noble Brahmin,
Extended blessing to Krishna and Arjuna.

12.77

Many times, the mother and father,
Gathered and lifted their sons,
They were wiping the happy tears,
Flowing from their eyes,
They were feeding them -
Milk, unrefined sugar and pudding,
And to the relative's homes,
The Brahmin was taking them, to show.

12.78

After having bowed to the Brahmin,
Very pleased with recovering his sons,
Lord Krishna, along with Arjuna,
Who had accomplished what was needed,
Lived happily in Dwaraka,
Tending to the needs of his beautiful wives,
And, he the remover of the woes of the ailing,
Krishna, the essence of the Vedas, lived joyfully,

12.79

Having lessened the burdens of the world,
And gracefully provided for the welfare,
Of Brahmins and the like; and one who can,
With equal measure, increase wealth and virtue,
With Satyabhama, Rukmini and others,
Krishna in happiness lived at Dwaraka.
May Krishna, grant material and spiritual bliss,
Those like you and me, the lowly ones to gain.

12.80

This text, which is about the playful, revered,
Stories of Krishna is chaste in its presentation,
If one accepts, this to be the main path,
Towards gaining divine blessing,
Then, spiritual wisdom will stay in his inner mind;
All misfortunes will vanish; he be liked by others;
Become famous; acquire good reputation;
And he will gain spiritual salvation as well.

about the translator

Ram Varmha hails from Kerala. At a young age, he emigrated to the US to pursue higher studies in engineering and management. Subsequently, he worked with organizations such as Ford Motor Co. and IBM, in engineering and management positions.

Despite residing overseas, Varmha continued to be close to his Indian heritage and studied and translated old Sanskrit texts. In 1977, he translated from Sanskrit to English the famed *Narayaneeyam*, a 16th-century text dedicated to Sri Krishna of the Guruvayur Temple, by the great Kerala sage, Sri Melpathur Narayana Bhattathiri. Varmha was the first to transcribe this renowned text in English and copies have since been accepted into many leading libraries in the US.

Varmha belongs to the ruling family of the erstwhile State of Cochin. Now retired, he and his wife, Uma, spend their time in the US and India.

www.ingramcontent.com/pod-product-compliance
Lightning Source LLC
Chambersburg PA
CBHW071425090426
42737CB00011B/1570